Conversational Regression

An (H)NLP Approach to Reimprinting Memories

NLP Mastery Series

By

Jess Marion

Changing Mind Publishing
New York, NY

Changing Mind Publishing
New York, NY

Conversational Regression
NLP Mastery Series
©Copyright 2016 Jess Marion and Changing Mind Publishing.

For further information, please contact Changing Mind Publishing, 545 8th Avenue, Suite 930, New York, N.Y. 10018

Cover Design by Richie Williamson
Editing by Wendell Anderson

Contents

Chapter 1
Welcome to Reimprinting

As you begin this book, you are stepping through a portal that can transport you and your clients across space and time. What would it be like if you could change the past so that the present and future become greater than anything you could have expected before now? Reimprinting is a powerful NLP technique that allows your clients to do just that—to rewrite their own history in ways that will generate positive change throughout the rest of their lives. As you explore these pages, I ask that you hold one presupposition in mind. This one belief, which comes from John Overdurf's (H)NLP, will transform your client work. The presupposition is simple: "Reality is a construction." We explore this in more depth in chapter 3. For now, feel comfortable in knowing that when you hold this belief, you have the ability to choose the reality you want for your own life, and it removes any limitations you may be tempted to put on a client's ability to succeed in the coaching or hypnosis session.

As you go forward through this book, you will see references to both hypnosis and coaching sessions. In my map of the world, they are the same. If you are doing a reimprinting, you are doing hypnosis because by its very nature, this pattern elicits trance and hypnotic phenomena. With that said, you may be coming from a strictly coaching perspective with no prior hypnosis training, and you can certainly rest assured that you will be able to use this pattern with ease. If you come from a formal hypnosis background, you will find the conversational nature of this technique fascinating. And it can certainly be adapted to a more traditional approach to hypnotherapy.

Thought Experiment

What would it be like if you were able to travel through time and change anything in the past that, when changed, would have a positive impact on you today? Carefully consider the events of your life. What if you could feel different about a memory? How much more empowering would it be for you to be free of any negative associations with that memory? It doesn't have to be anything big—it could be as small as letting go of some discomfort for the past. The interesting thing is small changes in the past can lead to profound transformations today.

Take a moment and make yourself comfortable. For this experiment, I'm going to invite you to begin to play with the nature of memories. An easy way to do this is to begin by relaxing comfortably and taking a few comfortable breaths.

Now call to mind a memory that, when you think about it now, may cause some mild unease, and you would like to feel different about it. Choose a memory that has a noticeable negative feeling; not one, however, that is incredibly strong. While the pattern you are learning in this book is designed for big emotional states, this is just a thought experiment, so make it easy for you.

Once you have the memory and feel the emotion, step outside of it so that you could view it almost as though you were watching a movie. See yourself in it and anyone else who may have been there. Yet you, as the adult, can watch it in a dissociated manner. Make that movie small and place it down on the floor. Take a moment to notice how the feeling about that memory now changes with it small and on the floor.

As you see that younger self in that scene on the floor, if you could gift that self any emotional resource that would make a difference for you now, what would it be? I'm not talking necessarily about a cognitive understanding but an emotion that would make a difference for that younger self in the scene. What is it like when you experience that emotion in the present? You may recall the last time and place that you felt that positive state and notice what it's like to feel it in your body. Allow yourself to fully step into this positive emotion and really feel it from the inside out. You may notice that the emotion has a color, a temperature, or a movement. Become aware of any aspect of that state that helps to increase the good feelings.

Once you feel this state fully and completely, send it to the younger self in that scene on the floor. Everyone has a different way of doing this. Some people imagine the color of the emotion flowing from themselves into the memory; others imagine it as an energetic transfer. Whatever way your unconscious mind chooses to do this is just the right way.

Once that emotion has entered the memory and has helped the younger self, watch that memory play again, and notice how it is different now. Become aware of how it feels to see this memory play out now that that younger self has access to that positive state.

If you would like to play with this a bit more, choose another positive state that would make the difference for you now. Step into that emotion, and gift it to the younger self. You can do this with as many states as needed.

Consider also that if there were other people involved in that memory, they too were probably not at their most resourceful. You could run the same pattern, gifting them resourceful states that would make the difference for you now.

For example: Perhaps a parent needed more flexibility or a classmate more compassion.

Watch the memory play out again, and notice how it is different this time. If you are already to the point of feeling comfortable, and you feel it's appropriate, you could step into the memory with a first-person view, getting to feel how things are different now.

When you are ready, allow the memory to drift back from where it came, knowing that you have the ability to change your feelings and the impact of memories in the present moment.

You may have noticed some very interesting changes in the emotions around this memory. Some people will notice that the emotional charge of the old memory has faded and they're now comfortable with it. Others may become aware of a more neutral feeling towards the memory. Finally, others may feel a slight decrease in the emotions surrounding the memory. In any case, you've had an important experience of the nature of memory. Keep this in mind as you continue in this book.

Regression: A Brief History

Regression has long been an important part of hypnotherapeutic history. Over the years, a number of highly respected hypnotists have left their indelible marks on this technique. In this section, I present a brief and broad overview of some of the key figures in the history of hypnotic regression work.

Freudian Regressions

One of the earliest accounts of the use of hypnotic regression comes from Sigmund Freud in the late 19th century. Hypnosis was an important part of Freud's therapeutic practice early in his career. In one of his published papers, he presented the case study of a woman named Anna who was suffering from partial paralysis. Freud used hypnotic regression as the main tool in relieving her symptoms.

Despite a few case studies available, Freud had limited success with hypnosis as a whole and very quickly abandoned its practice in exchange for his psychoanalytical approach.

Although he abandoned formal hypnosis, Freud had developed a theory of the mind, which supposed the subconscious mind is the reservoir of our dreams, memories, and drives. Most of these things are *repressed* and kept out of conscious awareness. They can, however, manifest in psychological and physical issues.

Freud abandoned hypnosis yet was still interested in the repressed memories of his clients. He would elicit these memories through hours of psychoanalysis. He found a number of his clients reporting memories of sexual abuse from childhood. He theorized that these were not, in fact, memories of what actually happened; instead, they were mental constructs representing the deeply buried sexual drives of the client or, in some cases, an expression of Oedipal complex. Once could certainly argue that psychoanalysis, as a practice, elicited trances and perhaps functioned as a hypnotic process. However, Freud himself would most likely disagree.

While Freud's theories are typically not embraced by the hypnosis and coaching communities, he is recognized as an important marker in the history of regression work.

Erickson and Regressions

Milton Erickson is a pivotal figure in the history of hypnosis both for his contribution of indirect hypnotic techniques and for the introduction of hypnosis into modern medicine and therapy. Throughout his career, he utilized regression work extensively. Sometimes the regression was covert, for example, the *Early Learning Set*. In this approach, he would choose a universal childhood experience and indirectly associate the client into the experience, thus regressing him. The universal experience, such as learning to read or ride a bike, became a parallel reality to the client's problem, which allowed Erickson to do therapy through the metaphor of the experience.

For example: He might encourage the client to go back to the earliest memories of walking and the experience of looking at the world from a different perspective. That experience became a resource for taking a different perspective with the client's issue.

Other times he would use direct hypnosis to send the client back into a past event and then proceed to introduce new information and resources. The most well-known use of this type of regression by Erickson was the subject of the book *The February Man*. In this complete transcript of a therapeutic intervention, Erickson worked with a young woman who suffered from a severe phobia and depression. Over multiple sessions, Erickson regressed her to different meaningful points in her history, including her birthdays (in February). Erickson then stepped into the memories as a trusted friend and adviser, and coached the client through the different stages of her life. The result of this was a complete transformation of the client.

Although trained in Freudian psychology, Erickson was a revolutionary in the field thanks to his view of the unconscious mind. While Freud viewed it as a dark and dangerous place, Erickson took a very different stance. He fully believed that the unconscious mind is the repository of all of our life experiences. And even more than that, it is the source of all resourcefulness. He believed the unconscious mind deserves a tremendous amount of respect and the more a client could create a positive relationship between the conscious and unconscious, the easier it was for the client to change.

Erickson's unflinching positive regard for the unconscious mind filters through hypnosis today. As we go forward, you may find it useful to really know that you have an unconscious mind that makes learning easy and transformation possible.

Classical Hypnotic Regression Work

During Erickson's time, there was another branch of hypnosis coming into its own in the modern era that focused on the use of rapid inductions and direct suggestions. Although labeled *classical hypnosis*—meaning reflecting the original tradition of hypnosis as found in the works of greats such as Braid and Esdale—classical hypnosis went through a renaissance in the mid-20th century. Hypnotists, including the legendary Gil Boyne and his contemporaries, utilized direct suggestion combined with the *affect bridge* (which we explore later) to take clients back to the *initial sensitizing experience*, the ISE, to release emotions and let go of the problem.

In this type of regression work, and hypnosis as a whole, it is clear that the hypnotist is guiding the experience and the client is moved through a specific procedure where little variation is required. This approach is very popular today among some hypnotists and has become a part of the curriculum of some hypnosis schools.

Leary, Dilts, and NLP Reimprinting

While Erickson expected the unconscious mind of the individual to make all of the changes necessary in its own way, NLP took a slightly different approach. Keep in mind that NLP developed through modeling. In the case of therapy, it was modeling the likes of Erickson, Satir, and Perlz. The result of this was the codification of different therapeutic processes into uniform steps. The steps were implemented by the coach, who would then calibrate the client's response and then adjust the intervention accordingly.

In the early 1980s Robert Dilts became interested in Timothy Leary both as a thinker and as someone who had a tremendous ability to learn and integrate ideas and techniques rapidly. Leary and Dilts spent countless hours discussing reality, the brain, and human potential. One area of particular interest for Leary was the relationship between childhood memories (or imprints) and how they effected humans as we grow into adults. Both Leary and Dilts were particularly interested in the work of Konrad Lorenz who first observed memory imprints in ducks. Lorenz discovered that in the first day of life ducklings form imprints for their mother that help them to learn and navigate their world. In one experiment ducklings were presented with a balloon during the imprint phase. They took the balloon as the mother, following it around as the researched pulled it. This imprint had a catastrophic effect on the ducks as adults. They did not find mates, have ducklings, or engage in typical social behavior. The memory imprint drastically altered the life trajectory of the ducks.

Leary believed that humans have imprints as well that are linked to certain biological states. Unlike ducks however, we are neurologically sophisticated and if we access certain states we are able to alter negative imprints in ways that change our lives now.

Leary and Dilts worked together to create the NLP Reimprinting pattern. This technique relies on the elicitation of states and the use of *spatial anchoring*. The Leary-Dilts approach to reimprinting involves having the client walk her timeline as she associates into a memory or disassociates from it.

For example: A client who had a traumatic childhood event can literally walk back into that event and experience it from the inside out. Or she could step off her timeline and interact with the event from a dissociated point of view. The client changes the memory and her relationship with the memory by gifting resources to herself and the other actors in the event. Then when it's time to reintegrate, the client can walk from that memory point on her timeline fully associated and move all the way up to the present moment.

Overdurf and Conversational Change

Building on the Leary-Dilts model for reimprinting, John Overdurf transitions it from an overt process into a conversation. While the core of the process—the use of association and dissociation with resourcing—remains intact, the Overdurf approach does not ask the client to walk his timeline. Instead, spatial anchoring is done through gesture while dissociation is achieved through submodality shifts. This makes the pattern even more user friendly and versatile.

This book explores Overdurf's approach to reimprinting in depth, as opposed to the Dilts model. The reasoning for this is that the conversational approach is more easily utilized in a wide variety of settings. The framing of it as well allows the reimprinting to be as overt or as covert as the coach desires. Without walking the timeline, the client may have less conscious awareness that a coaching strategy is being employed, which, in turn, may be more useful for him as well as for you as the coach.

The Four Steps of the Reimprinting Technique

1. *Association*: Associate the client into the negative state to access the memory to be reimprinted.
2. *Dissociation*: Once the memory is active, help your client to dissociate from the emotions by placing the memory on the floor, changing its submodalities, and changing how you speak about the memory.
3. *Resourcing*: Associate the client into resource states, and invite him to resource the younger self, followed by anyone else in the memory and anyone who should have been there but who wasn't.
4. *Association*: Associate the client into the new memory to experience it from the inside out. Use association only when appropriate.

In This Book

As with the other NLP Mastery Series books, this book presents you the reimprinting pattern in depth so that you can begin using it immediately. From there, I will present a number of variations on regression work to give you the greatest amount of flexibility with your clients.

Please note that from this point forward, I will be using *regression* and *reimprinting* interchangeably, so rest assured should you see either word appear, I am speaking about the same thing unless otherwise noted.

As you continue in this book, keep in mind that reimprinting is a highly transformative tool that helps clients to change their lives. When Erickson and Rossi wrote *The February Man,* they subtitled it "Evolving Consciousness and Identity in Hypnotherapy." I think that was a very apt description of this type of work. We are helping our clients to evolve into people living their lives according to their highest values. For many clients, this is about stepping into the identity they have always wanted for themselves but were held back because of past events or learnings that are no longer resourceful for them.

Chapter 2
Reimprinting Demonstration

In this chapter, you will find a transcript from a session in which reimprinting was the main modality used to help the client change. Some details might grab your attention from the beginning, including the absence of a formal trance induction.

The client was a 20-year-old university student who had been raised in a community where hypnosis was seen as evil. Although he was open to it and desperate to change, his unconscious cues made it clear that I would have to do a lot more work around hypnosis if it were to overtly use it. This illustrates the point that reimprinting is not only conversational but allows easy elicitation of hypnotic phenomena in any depth of trance.

This client's presenting issue was a fear of vomiting. He was the primary parent of a 2-year-old girl. He was afraid of the vomit and had created a meta-fear around not being able to take care of his child. He also worried that she would inherit his fear.

This transcript picks up after the initial intake.

> Coach: So tell me, James, about the last time and place you experienced this fear.

Client: It was last week. I was at home taking care of my little girl.

Coach: What's happening?

Client: She doesn't feel well, and I'm afraid she might vomit. [The client's physiology shows that he has fully associated into the moment.]

Coach: This is not the first time you have felt this fear, is it?

Client: No.

Coach: What is that earlier instance you are thinking about now?

Client: I'm in my dorm room, and my buddy had too much to drink last night. [At this point, the client is fully in the problem trance.]

Coach: This is not the first time you have had this feeling either, is it?

Client: No.

Coach: Allow the scene to fade and the emotion to take you even further back now. [The coach waits to see the unconscious cue that a memory has been found.]

Coach: Where are you?

Client: I'm in school.

Coach: What grade are you in?

Client: Fifth.

Coach: What's happening now?

Client: I don't feel well. I'm scared I'll be sick and everyone will laugh.

Coach: Is that the first time you felt that way? [The coach uses past tense language to begin dissociating the client.]

Client: No.

Coach: Drift back to that first time now. Put that memory on the ground. [Coach gestures to the client's past.] Make it small and dim. You can see little James there in the memory. Does that James have a nickname?

Client: Yes, Jimmy.

Coach: As you see little Jimmy there, is he alone or with others?

[Client's physiology shifts out of the regressed state and into his more neutral way of being.]

Client: He's with his mom and aunt.

Coach: Is there anyone who should have been there who wasn't?

Client: No one.

Coach: What's happening in that scene down there? [The coach gestures to the same point on the floor keeping her gestures low to the ground.]

Client: I'm scared. [The client is trying to associate back into the memory.]

Coach: What was little Jimmy afraid of? [The coach helps him dissociate by referring to the memory in third person and mismatching the language.]

Client: He sees his aunt is sick and his mom is upset. He's really worried about her.

Coach: Is this when little Jimmy learned to have that fear?

Client: Yes.

Coach: What an amazing little boy Jimmy is for caring so much about his family.

Client: Yes. [He smiles slightly as breathing relaxes signaling the unconscious mind's acceptance of the reframe.]

Coach: Let's help little Jimmy through this experience. What inner resources do you have now that little Jimmy could have used in that moment?

Client: Knowing that his aunt is going to be all right in a few hours.

Coach: And you have had a wealth of experiences with that aunt since that memory, correct? [The coach knew this to be true from the beginning of the session.]

Client: Yes. In fact, I saw her last week at a family party. [The client's physiology moves from neutral to resourceful.]

Coach: How wonderful! I'd like you to send that knowledge into the memory over there. Let little Jimmy know that he is going to have so many good times with his aunt and she'll feel better soon. I don't know if you'll send it energetically. Maybe you'll whisper in little Jimmy's ear, or your unconscious can find any other way to send this message that is appropriate for you. [Coach sees a head nod once the process is complete.] Now watch that memory and notice how it is different. How has it changed?

Client: Little Jimmy is not as afraid. He is still unsure, though, about what is happening.

Coach: What other resources do you have that little Jimmy could have used that will make the difference in that situation?

Client: Calmness.

Coach: And you know what it's like to be really calm, do you not? You could find many happy memories of being calm throughout your life and then begin to deepen your sense of calm. Or you could allow the deepening feeling of calmness to bring to mind many other memories of calm. And as you're curious as to which way that will happen, calmness can grow in its own way for you.

[Client drifts into a closed-eye trance.]
And you may even get a sense of the color of calmness and allow that to flow into the memory. Now watch the memory again and notice how it has changed.

Client: It's more distant and Jimmy is fine.

Coach: That's right; he is fine, calm, and really knows that everything will be fine. Is there anything else he needs in order for you to be free?

Client: No.

Coach: Would you like to step back inside this memory and feel it from the inside out?

Client: Yes.

Coach: Go ahead and feel how this is different now. Be little Jimmy in that moment with the knowledge that everything is OK and feeling calm. [Coach waits a few moments.] And you can step out and open your eyes and see it back on the floor. How is it different now?

Client: It's a little strange. It's like I can see everything, but all of the old emotions are gone. I wasn't expecting it to be like that!

Coach: Congratulations for making this powerful change in your life! Would you like to continue turning this memory into something you can really use to change your life?

Client: Absolutely!

Coach: How about those other people in that memory? What skills or resources do you have now that they could have used?

Client: My mom needs to not panic.

Coach: [Coach suspects that the client's fear was learned from the mother.] When she's not panicking, how is she being?

Client: She's calm.

Coach: And I know you know what it's like to be calm as you can recall those feelings you had just a moment ago as that calm deepens. And you know what to do.

Client: Yes.

Coach: And it's interesting because little Jimmy knows a lot more about being calm too, so I wonder what will happen when this memory plays and Mom sees Jimmy being calm knowing that everything will be OK? I'm curious what Mom will learn. [Coach creates a loop by not only sending calmness to the mother but also has the mother learn from the little boy instead of the other way around as happened in the original imprinting.] What happens in that memory now?

Client: It's very different. I'm not afraid anymore.

Coach: That's right. I wonder how calming it can be to know that you are in control. Now, there is one other person in this memory who may need a resource you have. What does your aunt need? [The coach suggested the imprinting of the aunt because there may be a time in the future when the client or his daughter becomes ill, and reframing the aunt's experience will be empowering for the client in those future situations.]

Client: She needs comfort and to be reassured.

Coach: And you know what comfort is like.

Client: Yes.

Coach: It's interesting; there are two types of comfort. First, there is the physical experience of comfort where you can remember those instances where you feel comfort. Allow your mind to bring all of those memories of being comfortable forward because you can give your aunt the gift of comfort by reminding her what it is like to feel comfort. Now, the second type of comfort is on another level. It comes from kind words and brings about calm and peace. I wonder how you might now gift that to her. If you were to watch that memory now, how has it changed?

Client: It's getting harder to see. I just feel calm and relaxed.

Coach: It really is getting harder to see. And as you are calm and relaxed, would you like to step into this one more time?

Client: Yes.

Coach: You can do that now as you integrate the new learning. And, of course, your unconscious mind can, outside of your conscious awareness, make changes to all of those other instances where you can now be calm, in control comforted by the knowledge that everything is OK. And as that happens, you can grow up through that experience, through your school days when you are calm and into your teenage years and through college until you are you are your full age. That was some experience!

Client: Yea, I wasn't expecting that!

Coach: Isn't it comforting to know that you can make changes like this easily and quickly? Now we can help to solidify the change even further by just closing your eyes for a moment and imagining you're in a place that makes your feel safe and calm. It could be somewhere you know in your daily life or somewhere your mind creates. Either way is better because you are going to use this space to make lasting change on a deep level. It may be a weird thing to think about, but there were people in your past who were doing the best they could but may have helped to maintain those old emotions. For example: Your mom did the best she could, and yet there may be things that you would like to say to her in this space as you forgive anything that needs forgiving as you fully let go of that old issue. So take a moment and invite her into this space, saying whatever you need to say to her for you to move forward. ... That's right. Now there may be someone else such as your aunt. You can invite her in and say what needs to be said as your forgive her and let go. You may consciously think there is no forgiveness needed, and you would be right to rest assured knowing that this is an important step for you. ... Very good. As she leaves this space, is there anyone else who needs to be forgiven for having any involvement with that old issue?

Client: Yes, the kids at school.

Coach: So invite them in one at a time and say whatever needs to be spoken for you to fully enjoy your new freedom. ... That's it. Is there anyone else?

Client: No.

Coach: Might I suggest one more person, the most important person?

Client: [Nods head.]

Coach: Little Jimmy. He did the best he could throughout your life to keep you safe and happy. He was so loving as a small boy that he reacted the only way he knew how in that moment. Invite him in and thank him for everything he did for you. Let him know what a good job he did. .... That's right. ... Take all of the time you need to do this. When you're ready, give him a hug, let him melt into you, become a part of you. ... You're doing a great job. Now, there will be a time in the future when you are around someone who is vomiting, maybe your daughter or someone else. What happens?

Client: I take care of them and help them until they feel better.

Coach: And how do you feel in that moment?

Client: I'm not noticing, just taking care of that person. I feel fine.

Coach: Check in with your body. How do you know you are doing fine?

Client: I can feel it.

Coach, That's right. And there may be a time in the future when you are the one having the experience. What happens?

Client: It doesn't feel good, but I'm OK.

Coach: You are absolutely right. It's not supposed to be pleasant, but you know that you are going to be all right. ... Go to another time in the future where you are healthy and happy and maybe a stranger gets sick. What happens?

Client: I help if I can. Everything is all right.

Coach: Very good, and you can rest comfortably knowing that the changes you have made here today will continue to generalize and grow. Even tonight as you sleep and dream, your unconscious is fully integrating this change on a deep, deep level. ... Now, only as slowly as you allow this change to take root will your eyes open and you can fully come back to the here and now. ... Welcome back! So talk to me about that old fear again.

Client: I don't have it anymore!

Coach: Are you sure? [Said teasingly.]

Client: Yes, it's gone.

Coach: How do you know?

Client: I just do.

Coach: Think about someone being sick and notice how your body feels. How does it feel?

Client: Calm, relaxed.

Coach: Are you sure? You mean you've changed? You're not just saying that are you? [Teasing a bit more forcibly.]

Client: Yes. I feel good!

Two weeks after this session, the client reported that the fear was completely gone and that his life had changed in a powerfully positive way because of it.

In the upcoming chapters we explore the neuroscience behind this pattern so that you can use it with confidence. And we dive deeply into the mechanics of it so that it is easy to implement immediately.

Chapter 3
The Neuroscience of Reimprinting

It was once a popular belief that memories were stored in the brain like static video or files on a desktop. When you recalled something, it was simply a matter of opening the file and experiencing the memory. The consequence of this model was the belief that memories are first an accurate recording of actual events and secondly that they were unchanging. Fortunately, research in psychology and neuroscience has found that memory is far more flexible than at one time believed. Memories can be distorted, implanted, and dramatically altered.

As you will discover in this chapter, memory is a fluid process that relies on a system of associations between neural networks. Neural networks are plastic—so are memories. In this chapter, I introduce you to key concepts in current scientific thinking surrounding memory encoding and the process of reconsolidation. This will provide you with a more refined understanding of why and how reimprinting works as a therapeutic process.

Before we can explore how to actively change memories, let's begin by examining how memories are encoded and consolidated. There are different types of encoding processes in the brain, depending on the type of memory being created.

Broadly speaking, we can divide memories into *explicit memories* and *implicit memories*. Explicit memories are memories that contain some level of conscious involvement in the retrieval process. Implicit memories do not contain conscious awareness. They tend not to have a tremendous amount of conscious information associated with them.

For our purposes, we are interested primarily in episodic memory. The information presented in this chapter pertains specifically to the encoding of this type of memory.

Explicit and Implicit Memory

Long-Term Memory Type	Memory Function
Explicit	Conscious awareness that something is being remembered
Semantic	Data and facts
Episodic	Autobiographical
Implicit	No conscious awareness that something is being remembered
Priming	Information that lacks explicit memory can still influence thoughts and behavior
Procedural	Automatic behaviors not requiring conscious awareness

Explicit memories are what we typically think of when we think about memories; they contain the vast amounts of information about ourselves and the world around us that our brain thought important enough to keep.

Explicit memory can be divided further into two categories, *semantic* and *episodic*. Semantic memory is the recall of facts and figures. At some point you learned a fact, and it was either novel enough for you to encode it quickly or you spent time memorizing it.

For example: In school, you may have committed to memory the capital of Chile or the answer to 5×5. At some point, you would have learned these answers. However, now the memory of learning them is far less important than the information itself.

The second type of explicit memory, episodic memory, has to do with the things that you experience throughout your life. These memories create the story of you.

For example: You could recall a favorite vacation and some of the specific activities on a vacation or whom you were with. The images, sounds, and feelings that come to mind are contained within this form of episodic memory.

The second classification of memories is *implicit*. These types of memories are experiences outside of conscious awareness. While you remember a lovely holiday, you normally know you are experiencing a memory. When an implicit memory is active, you typically don't realize it.

Classification for implicit memories is not as clear-cut as their semantic and episodic counterparts. Implicit memory is often observed in two roles, priming and procedure.

Priming is the principle that information that has already been presented to the individual can influence thoughts and behaviors later even though the person does not have conscious recollection of the information or any explicit memory to accompany it.

Procedural memory is connected with unconscious behaviors. These are the things you do automatically and usually don't even have conscious awareness that you are doing them.

For example: If you drive a car, you probably don't think much about how you do it; you just sit in the car and drive. Any type of behavior that doesn't require conscious energy, that you automatically do, occurs because it was encoded as a procedural memory.

While explicit memories are encoded and consolidated in the hippocampus, research suggests that procedural memories are consolidated in the neocortex. These types of memories are consolidated over multiple repetitions of the behavior.

If we think about our coaching clients who come in for therapeutic change, they are often feeling something that they don't want to feel or behaving in an unresourceful way. Explicit memory is connected to the emotional states that the client does not want to feel as well as all of the episodes in the past when the problem was experienced. Procedural memory is connected to unconscious habits, for example, the smoker who has no conscious perception of lifting up the cigarette and smoking throughout the day.

The main reimprinting pattern presented in this book focuses on changing episodic memories that will, in turn, change states and behaviors.

(In the last portion of this book, I present a number of variations on reimprinting, one of which will allow you to help clients reconsolidate procedural memories.)

For the remainder of this chapter, I focus on the encoding, consolidation, and reconsolidation of episodic memories.

Encoding

The first step of memory creation, encoding, happens through attention and unconscious processing. As information comes in through your sensory channels, your brain makes a split-second decision whether or not the sensory information is important enough to increase your attention. It does this by processing the sensory information in the amygdala first. The amygdala is responsible for processing the emotional component of the event. The greater the emotion, the more intense the attention becomes, which, in turn, incites neurons to fire more frequently increasing the likelihood that the event will be transformed into a memory. The role of the amygdala in episodic memory encoding is so important that studies have shown damage to the amygdala impairs the brain's ability to give the required amount of attention for the encoding of emotional events.

If we think of the brain as a complex system of pathways similar to a subway system, through which information travels, the amygdala is the first stop for sensory information on the memory-encoding train. Once the information has been processed by the amygdala, the sensory systems in the brain become active. These are primarily the auditory, visual, kinesthetic, and semantic systems. The olfactory system plays a role as well; however, the precise mechanism for this aspect of encoding is not entirely clear. While three of the four active systems are dedicated to the sensory component of the memory, semantic processing assigns the meaning to the memory.

All of the systems are in active communication with the hippocampus, where the memory trace is formed and will eventually be consolidated. The hippocampus's job is to take all of the sensory information, including the meaning of the event, and form it into one cohesive representation. This representation is often called a *memory trace* or *engram*. It is believed that these are biochemical events; however, they have yet to be recorded through brain-imaging technology.

From here, the brain has some decisions to make. It may choose to keep the information in short-term memory, which means it will be readily available in the immediate future. Or it can be moved to long-term memory, which could last a lifetime.

Keep in mind that we are a meaning-making species. The brain is constantly looking for associations between new sensory information and previously stored information. Memory is associative. During the encoding process, while the memory is in the hippocampus, it will become associated with similar events and linked neurologically to networks where associations have been made.

Consolidation

The next step in long-term memory formation is the stabilization of the engram through the process of consolidation. Memory consolidation happens in two phases:

1. *Synaptic Consolidation*
2. *System Consolidation*

Synaptic Consolidation

This is the establishment of a new neural network associated with the memory. At this point, the memory links with other associated memories. This occurs through Hebb's Law. Hebb's Law states: "Neurons that fire together wire together," meaning that when two or more neurons or networks of neurons fire at the same time, they link together. The more frequently these networks fire together, the stronger the links become until they are wired together.

The newly formed memory begins to form links with other neural networks in the brain, and each time those networks fire simultaneously they become more sensitive. Synaptic consolidation wires the memory into the brain and may rewire other memories and associated networks. Keep in mind that although I'm speaking about a memory creating a physical structure in the brain, neuroplasticity states that those networks are flexible and change over time or through the introduction of new information.

System Consolidation

The final stage of memory consolidation occurs over weeks and sometimes years. At this phase, the memory network is moved into the neocortex.

Example: To help you conceptualize this process in the real world, let's consider for a moment a hypothetical client who has a fear of dogs. This client sees a dog and feels intense fear. We could be curious as to how this fear developed. Perhaps when he was a young boy, he walked by a yard that had a big dog that barked at him. The sound of the bark went in through the auditory system and was filtered by the amygdala, which decided on the feeling of fear. Through evolution, the startle reflex has been hardwired to loud sounds in the human brain.

Once the amygdala has decided on the state, the boy's attention will have been completely drawn towards the dog. Every sensory system associated with memory encoding will have become active; the rest of the sensory information begins to be processed, including the image of the dog. A semantic meaning is also assigned; perhaps it is "that was scary." All of this information is filtered into the hippocampus, which begins the process of wiring the sensory information to other networks with similar information, perhaps other networks associated with dogs.

If the emotional response was strong enough, the consolidation process would have begun within minutes of the initial event.

That memory may have been strong enough to create the lasting fear, depending on the way in which the memory was wired into the brain, including the semantic meaning given to it. Or it may take another instance of the boy encountering a dog; maybe this time it's a little dog that snaps at him. The event will have gone through the amygdala, which assigned fear once again, and the encoding process will have begun all over. This time the new memory gets linked with the first memory of the dog, and perhaps the new meaning that's made is "all dogs are scary."

Then again there is a third negative experience that when consolidated joins the network of "dogs are scary." Now the new meaning is "fear keeps me safe from dogs." The brain has now learned that when the client sees a dog, he can be afraid, and based on experiences in the past, he survives the event. Now a new pathway is created in the brain that goes from seeing dogs to feeling fear as a survival mechanism for the client.

Our job as coaches and hypnotists is to help rewire the client's brain so that he can make new meanings of those events.

Encoding and Consolidation Interruption

During the encoding and consolidation process, the memory is highly unstable. New information can alter and distort the memory. A common example of this is the interruption of the encoding of short-term memory when trying to recall a list. Most people have had the experience of trying to memorize a list or a phone number for short-term use. These types of short-term memories tend to be encoded verbally, and if any new verbal information is introduced, the encoding is interrupted, for example, if someone begins to speak with you as you're trying to memorize the list. A way to enhance your short-term memory skills is to encode the list visually.

Interruptions in the consolidation phase of long-term memories can also create lasting changes in those memories. This was discovered well before the advances in brain imaging technology through the research of Dr. Elizabeth Loftus. Over the last four decades, she has devoted her career to researching the flexibility of memory.

The Misinformation Effect

The *misinformation effect* arises when external information changes a memory during the consolidation process. This was first discovered in a groundbreaking study conducted by Loftus and Palmer in 1974. In this study, two groups of people watched video footage of the same car accident and were then asked questions about the accident immediately after. One group was asked the question, "About how fast were the cars going when they smashed into each other?" The second group was asked the same question however *smashed* was replaced by other verbs, such as *collided, bumped,* or *contacted.* It was found that the group exposed to the word *smashed* estimated the speed of the vehicles to be much higher than the group asked using the other words.

One week later both groups were asked if they saw broken glass in the accident. The "smashed" group was more likely to say yes to the question even though there was no broken glass in the video. ("Reconstruction of Automobile Destruction: An Example of the Interaction between Language and Memory," Loftus and Palmer 1974).

This study showed that in the encoding and consolidating of episodic events, outside information can alter the memory. While Loftus was interested in the applications of the misinformation effect in eyewitness testimonies in court cases, for coaches, this becomes an important principle when it comes to helping clients reconsolidate memories.

Reconsolidation

Once consolidation has occurred and the new neural networks are created, it would be easy to think that the memory becomes a permanent fixture in the brain. In reality, it does not. It is still as malleable as it was during the original consolidation process. Each time an episodic memory is reviewed in detail, a number of connections within the memory's neural network become active and the memory is processed once again through the hippocampus. When this occurs, additional information is added to the memory. This occurs because the brain is different at the time of reconsolidation than it was during the original consolidation.

Experiences, learnings, and other episodic memories are available for wiring into the memory. During the original consolidation, the amygdala is activated before the other sensory regions of the brain are. This means the emotional response is automatic at the moment of encoding. During reconsolidation, however, the amygdala is not the gatekeeper for consolidation. While the original consolidation is a *feedforward process*—meaning information comes into the senses and travels from the more ancient parts of the brain to the youngest parts of the brain; during reconsolidation, the person is using *feedback* or top-down processing and engaging in recall and meaning making and using the memory to elicit the emotional state.

Each time you step into a vivid memory that memory is active in your hippocampus—and it changes. For some people, the change may be in the content, remembering the details differently. For others, it could be in the meaning of the memory or the emotions attached. Thanks to reconsolidation, we can literally rewrite our past.

Reconsolidation and Reimprinting

Reimprinting uses the principle of reconsolidation to transform memories. It is an active process through which the problematic memory is revivified, thus sending it back through the hippocampus. This time, instead of the memory being consolidated into a "problem" neural network, we attach it to a much bigger resource network. This is done by activating networks associated with strong resource states and applying those to the memory. As this happens, the meaning of the memory (the semantic information) is also transformed. The brain makes a new meaning out of the memory. In the example of the client afraid of dogs, the new semantic meaning might become "I'm comfortable."

Reimprinting interrupts the consolidation process in a positive way. It functions in the same way as the *Misinformation Effect* does during initial consolidation of memories. The only difference is that we use misinformation to influence the reconsolidation process in a highly positive manner.

It is essential in the second half of the reimprinting pattern to associate the client into resource states that she already has experience with. In the original study conducted by Loftus, it wasn't merely the word *smashed* that disrupted the encoding/consolidation of the memory; it was all of the neural networks and associations, inside the subjects' minds connected with the word. Likewise, we utilize the

Misinformation Effect in reimprinting to activate neural networks much larger than the individual memory.

Because the reconsolidation occurs in the coaching environment, we also have the opportunity to heavily leverage Hebb's Law. In the initial encoding, the brain relied on Long Term Potentiation to create the initial neural sensitivity then Hebb's Law took over resulting in the creation and strengthening of networks associated with the problem. The neural connections were reinforced each time the client thought about the memory and felt bad, or experienced something in the outside world that triggered the emotional response links to the memory.

For example: Our imaginary client may see a dog and feel fright; he may or may not consciously recall the initial learning of the fear of dogs. However, he has had a lifetime of practicing and strengthening those neural networks.

Something to keep in mind as well is that over time, people grow the problem network by creating a *meta-problem*. A meta-problem is typically feeling negatively and creating unresourceful semantic meanings about the fact she has a problem. This often takes the form of feeling embarrassed or discouraged because of the problem. So a client who has a phobia might be embarrassed of the phobia.

The other type of emotion is typically fear over experiencing the problem. *For example*: A client who has a fear of flying will typically also have a fear of displaying the fear reaction in public. The client has spent a lot of time and energy on strengthening those neural pathways, and now they have grown it by adding meta-emotions to the mix.

In reimprinting, we have the opportunity within a short period to build new neural connections and reinforce those through conditioning and practice. The key is help the client leverage resourceful neural networks which are more robust in state and semantic meaning than the problem network.

Chapter 4
The Memory Metaphor

Even though reimprinting is a powerful tool for transformation, a number of limiting beliefs among some practitioners stop them from effectively using this process with their clients and for themselves. In this chapter, I address some of the most common limiting beliefs so that you can move forward confidently learning and using this process.

Finding the ISE

One of the major concerns that many regression practitioners have is finding the *initial sensitizing event*, or ISE. They worry whether they dig deep enough into a client's past to find the ISE; otherwise, the change may not take. Speaking from the perspective of neuroscience and what we know about how memory works, there is no evidence supporting the necessity or even the possibility of finding an objective and accurate ISE. Memory reconsolidation first and foremost ensures that there is no possible way of knowing what the true ISE was. In fact, even if you find the original event, the odds are that the details recalled are not objectively accurate. The client has had any number of years of experience adding new information to that memory.

When doing a reimprinting, we invite the client to go back to an early memory of the problem. This is done for three reasons:

1. People are culturally programmed in the West to assign more significance to childhood memories, thanks to the influence of Freud on popular thinking. That alone creates a tremendous amount of belief by the client that what is being done "is real therapy," thus creating a tremendous amount of emotional leverage. When there is conviction, the placebo effect may also be present.

2. The neural pathways associated with the memory have had the most conditioning, and when we start to repurpose those connections, the metaphorical ground falls out from under the feet of the problem. There is also an unspoken implication that every other instance in the future will have to change in response.

3. We can use iteration throughout a number of memories to give the client ample opportunities to practice the change. If reimprinting is the main therapeutic modality, you can move forward through the client's timeline. Typically, after a handful of reimprintings (or sometimes even fewer), the problem dissolves. This is reminiscent of the Change Personal History Pattern.

It is important to note that going back to early memories is not always needed, especially when the client knows exactly when the problem started.

When you do go back to distant memories, trust the unconscious mind. Whatever memory is found by the unconscious is the right one to work with at this time. Ultimately, it is a metaphor. The client's unconscious mind is saying that this is the metaphor to use for this session. Think of regression work as a sophisticated use of the client's personal metaphors.

Aren't We Implanting False Memories?

The short answer is yes we are. I realize that some readers might be taken aback by that answer or even a bit concerned. I say yes because all memories have a level of falseness to them in that we don't recall things as they objectively occurred.

For example: We can take one of the few principles that is a law in psychology: State-Based Learning. Your emotional state at the moment of encoding impacts how the memory is encoded and influences how you recall an event. A student who is relaxed while learning but gets anxious during an exam will find it more difficult to access the information learned. This is because while the student is anxious, she is activating neural networks that have very few connections to the memories she has encoded while relaxed. The information might be distorted or deleted completely from the student's exam experience.

If you recall the Misinformation Effect, we purposefully implant "false" memories by introducing positive resource states. We change the neural networks associated with the problematic memory. This may or may not impact the content of the memory. And for our purposes, it does not matter. The regression work I am suggesting in this book is not about retrieving accurate information as a forensic hypnotist would. Instead, we are interested in changing the client's relationship to the memory. We facilitate the space for the client to safely explore and change the memory in a way that is resourceful for the client. The problematic memory is the metaphor the client has been using to keep the problem in place, and now we use that same metaphor to help the client create positive change.

What about Repressed Memories?

The concept of memory repression can trace its roots at least back to the time of Freud. Uncovering repressed memories and drives was a key part of psychoanalysis.

In the 1980s and '90s, there were a rash of accusations of abuse by people who had gone through various therapies that either purposefully or inadvertently unlocked "repressed" memories. These memories tore apart families and communities and brought criminal and civil proceedings to the alleged guilty parties. Sadly for all involved, these cases were often built on priming from sensationalized media reports and false episodic memory implantation by therapists. Unlike the "false" memories I spoke of in the previous section where we are interested in helping clients change their emotions, these therapists were looking for specific episodic memory content. Once "uncovered" that content was treated as being objectively accurate.

There is no scientific evidence to support the theory of repressed and recovered memories. There is, however, evidence of the ease of implanting false episodic memories.

In response to the legal proceedings in the 1990s, Elizabeth Loftus conducted a study in which researchers were able to implant false memories in subjects. In this case, the memory was being lost in a shopping mall as a child. The memory was implanted by first having subjects read four short anecdotes from their childhoods. Three of those stories were actual events (as confirmed by relatives before the study); one was the incident in the mall. The false story contained specific information that could have been correct, such as the name of the mall the subject would have visited as a child. This created plausibility in the minds of participants, which increased the likelihood that the event took place. To further implant the memory, the researchers asked a number of leading questions about all four events. After this process, 25 percent of subjects reported fully remembering the false event. They even began to fill in precise details about the false event.

The moral of the story here is to look at reimprinting as a modality for positive change. It is not to uncover repressed memories. While helping someone change the feelings and associations around memories will change the memories, using hypnosis or coaching techniques to uncover repressed memories runs the high risk of implanting negative false memories.

Is Regression Work Dangerous or Unnecessary?

While it may have seemed all doom and gloom in the above section, when done appropriately, reimprinting is a powerful and positive tool for change. It allows clients to rewrite their past in a way that empowers them to live the type of life they want today. Just like any other hypnosis or coaching tool, reimprinting can be used effectively or ineffectively. It comes down to your flexibility as a coach to hold the space for the client without adding too many of your own ideas. Your success will also depend on how you relate to your client (as is the case in all change work) and how you allow the client to explore the past in a comfortable and nonjudgmental way.

In terms of necessity, this really depends on you as a change-worker. Plenty of coaches don't do regressions for various reasons, yet they help their clients to change. The down side to this is it can be limiting for the coach and client. There are certain times during which the client's unconscious mind will tell you automatically that reimprinting is the best option at the moment. (I present those specific moments in the next chapter.) The question then becomes, Why not allow the client's unconscious to determine the direction and pace of the change?

Chapter 5
Key Times to Use Reimprinting

As mentioned in the previous chapter, there will be instances when the client's unconscious mind will tell you that a reimprinting is the approach to take. These suggestions come from John Overdurf's observations. I find them useful in my own practice. Perhaps you will as well.

1. The client tells you he knows exactly when the problem started (direct memory).

2. His physiology becomes regressed (the body doesn't lie).

3. The emotional response is out of proportion with the context (emotional energy).

These messages will show up in the client's words, tonality, and physiology. You may come from a background where you prefer to automatically do regression work, in which case, feel free to keep these three instances in mind for your own mental notes. Also feel free to use the process in this book whenever it's useful for your client.

You may be a practitioner, however, who selectively uses reimprinting, in which case, spotting these moments will make it easier for you to choose when and where to use it.

Direct Memory

In this instance, the client believes he knows exactly from where the problem comes. He has a specific memory in mind that serves as the starting point. As mentioned previously, we have no way of knowing whether the instance was the starting point. That matters little, however. The client has helped to maintain the problem by telling himself the narrative of that memory over and over again. In the past when he experienced the problem state or behavior, he may have thought to himself, "If it weren't for that, I wouldn't have this problem." Also, when experiencing the problem, that specific memory can be playing in the client's working memory (see "Keeping the Brain in Mind") in or out of conscious awareness, which helps to stabilize the issue. At other times, when the client is not experiencing the issue, he may be telling himself and others the narrative he has constructed around that memory. Whether the memory is fact or not, is the client still uses it to maintain the status quo.

There may be times when it is appropriate to go back before the memory the client presents. This is the case when the memory she is using most often to keep the problem in place is relatively recent.

For example: Someone with a phobia may be holding on to one event where she experienced the fear. However, she knows that she already had the fear before that point. In these cases, it is still important to work with the memories the client "consciously" offers. I say "consciously" because the information is obtained during the intake as opposed to the result of an affect bridge. Ultimately, though, it is the unconscious mind offering you a starting point. It is though the client were saying, "This memory is important to me in the context of the problem and needs to change." If you take a client back before the conscious memories of the problem, remember to also address the conscious memories so that you can help the client undo all of the working parts that held this in place in the past.

The Body Doesn't Lie

The body shows emotional states and internal representations far more quickly than the conscious mind perceives them. In fact, you can think of the body as a part of the unconscious mind. When you direct your conscious attention to some aspect of the body, you then have conscious control over it. The rest of the time it is the unconscious mind that is monitoring your physical experience.

For example: You could draw your attention to your left hand and make the conscious decision to lift it and to set it back down. As your conscious mind takes control of the arm, you may lose track of the fact that your eyes are still reading these words. Conscious awareness was focused on the hand while the unconscious mind was controlling the rest.

In the Free Will studies that Libet conducted in the 1980s, it was discovered that the body made choices before a subject consciously reported the choice and even before the portions of the brain linked to conscious recognition became active.

This is very evident during the coaching and hypnotic process. Your clients show their states and responses to your suggestions before they consciously report their experiences.

The same holds true when a client begins to associate into the problem state. In many instances, you will note the client's physiology matching the state.

For example: Someone who gets anxious may show you a physiology where she is fidgety, her breathing quickens, perhaps a change in skin tone is present, and other signs that let you know that something has changed within her experience. As a coach, either you will consciously recognize her responses or your unconscious mind automatically will pick up on them.

On some occasions, the physiology dramatically shifts. Instead of showing you the physiology of an adult experiencing the issue, the client automatically defaults to embodying the physiology of a child. As the client speaks about his problem, he may begin to swing his legs back and forth, shift in his seat, change his tonality and vocabulary. He is showing you an embodied version of his child self when he first encoded the problem state or behavior. The client, typically, does not consciously recognize he is doing this. To the coach, it is very clear. In these moments, the client has fully unconsciously associated into the moment of encoding. He may not even consciously realize the memory that's playing in his mind, but the body is expressing it for you.

If the association is full enough, you can even ask the client how old he is in this moment, and he will give you an age associated with the encoded event. Otherwise, you will know it because it will appear as though the client is growing younger in front of you on the level of behavior.

In these instances, the unconscious mind is telling you that this is an early learning that needs to be shifted. When the client is experiencing the problem in the outside world, he is experiencing a spontaneous regression. You can use the same mechanism to undo the issue.

Emotional Energy

The final category is closely linked with the second one in that these individuals will show you a regressed physiology. They, however, tend to take it a step further with a large emotional response. The emotional response is out of proportion with what is currently occurring. This does not necessarily even have a link consciously to what is being discussed or experienced. In its extreme form, it is often referred to as an *abreaction* (which I discuss later). In its more common form, it is a strong emotional response that could involve high levels of fear or tears. These can occur at, on the surface, what feels like a random moment. At the unconscious level, however, there is something that the client touched upon that is related to a bigger issue. Think of a child in an unresourceful state; that will give you some idea of what this looks like. When this occurs, the client loses touch with the present moment and her body relives the encoded experience.

These occurrences can happen at seemingly random moments. When they do occur, you have some options. The first is that you completely dissociate the client and reorient her into the here and now, making a choice to perhaps explore this later when more appropriate. Or you can use this as the jumping-off point into an issue that, once changed, will have a profoundly positive effect on the client. Keep in mind that if the client cannot dissociate enough to work with the memory, it becomes more useful and ecological to help her completely reorient to the outside world and find a more appropriate approach to helping the client change.

While these are certainly not the only times in which you can use reimprinting, they are the three instances that specifically lend themselves to the pattern of reimprinting. (I discuss what to do in all three instances in subsequent chapters.)

As mentioned above, you can feel free to use reimprinting with any client you choose. But having these three instances in mind will give your unconscious mind a road map when working with clients.

If you are still wondering what specific problems you should use reimprinting with, allow me to give some examples of the issues when I normally use reimprinting as a part of the change process. The most common instances are fears and phobias, smoking and other habits, traumatic events, and anxiety. In these instances, the client usually falls into one of the three categories discussed in this chapter.

Chapter 6
How Reimprinting Works

In this chapter, I give you a brief overview of the conversational reimprinting technique. In chapters 7 to 11, I go more in depth into the various steps.

Association and Memory Access

Begin by inviting the client to access the negative state she would like to change. This is done automatically by asking the client about what she wants to work through. At this point, decide if reimprinting is the path you both will take. As the client speaks about the issue, pay attention to whether she fits one of the three criteria described in the last chapter. If she does, the memory to be reimprinted may be immediately available to the client and you can associate her into the event. Other times, however, you will need to build an affect bridge (see chapter 7). This will allow you to jump back in time to the appropriate memory to be changed.

On the neurological level, you need to activate the neural networks associated with the problem so that the resource states you will be eliciting later have a place to connect. Remember that neurons that fire together wire together. You will also be sending the memory back through the hippocampus for reconsolidation.

Dissociating from the Memory

Once the memory has been elicited, pull the client out of it. It is important for the client to be placed into a position where he has the power to change the effects of the memory. Up to this point, the client has been experiencing the problem from the inside out. He has gotten caught up in the emotions and, at the very least, must wait the 60 seconds that it takes for the chemical wash connected to the emotion to run its course. More likely the feeling lasts longer because the client is doing something internally to keep it going. If the client experiences the problem state for only the 60-second duration, it is unlikely that he would be coming to see you for help, as it would not have enough of an emotional charge to motivate change.

Often when clients do step out of the problem state and observe it from the outside, they create a meta-issue where they now have feelings about having feelings in the context of the problem.

For example: A client who has a fear of flying feels bad when she plans to fly or step onto an airplane. The meta-problem is created when she thinks about her fear of flying and becomes worried about losing control of her emotions on the flight. Or she may think to herself that she shouldn't have the fear and she is being ridiculous. Either way her experience of the problem when outside of it in the past had helped to reinforce that issue.

During the reimprinting, we ask the client to step outside of the problem but into a position where ultimately she is empowered and in control. Instead of stepping out and reinforcing the problem, she can now step out and add resourceful feelings and behaviors to the old issue.

Resourcing the Memory

It's now time to change the memory. You do this by helping the client to associate into strongly positive states that he believes are needed in that situation. He will begin by resourcing himself. It may be that he needs one state or multiple states to change how he feels about and in the memory.

After resourcing the younger self, the client can resource the people present in the event, as well as anyone else who should have been there but was not. Between each person, if appropriate, the client can step in and out of the memory so that he has a number of reference experiences of the new emotions in the old context.

Integration

Once the experience of the memory has changed to one that is resourceful, the integration process can begin. This happens in two stages:

1. Invite (if appropriate) the client to step into the memory and experience it from the inside out. But this time lead her in growing up through the years until she is her present-day self. This unconsciously invites her to make this "new" memory a part of her continuing autobiography. There is an assumption that other events after this memory where the problem existed will inherently change.

2. Help the client generating forgiveness. This second stage can be a bit more difficult; nevertheless, is vital to the reconsolidation process. As long as the client holds onto the anger around the situation or the narrative of the situation itself, the integration can be more challenging. Therefore, you will want to encourage forgiveness through a formal visualization. This will allow the client to fully integrate the "new" memory into her life by dissolving any negative emotion that is meta to the event.

Iteration

After the memory has been reimprinted, lead the client through this process again, allowing her to add more resources to the event. Multiple iterations will have some fascinating results. The first is that if the client has a difficult time finding resources in the first round, as you go through it again, it becomes much easier. The other fortunate consequence is that the iteration acts as a compulsion blowout. Any remaining negative emotional energy will be exhausted.

Further Reimprinting

Let's take a trip back in time for a moment to the age of the Roman Empire. The Romans had their vision set on complete conquest of the known world, but they knew that they did not have the resources to continuously launch military attacks. They also realized that people were far more valuable as living citizens of the empire than they were as dead victims of war.

To build their empire, the Romans designed the perfect strategy. They would invade a town and burn it to the ground. They would, however, let a few people go, fully expecting those people to run off and tell the people in the next town what happened. When the survivors reached the next town, of course the townsfolk didn't believe them. Once again the Romans attacked, and once again they sent survivors to warn the next town. By the third or fourth town, people had heard what the Romans had done to their neighbors and surrendered without a fight. The Romans were able to conquer entire nations through minimal force.

While reimprinting one memory may be enough for some clients—especially those who believe the issue began with one specific event—it may not resolve the issue completely for others. Rest assured, though, the issue will have changed. In these instances, lead your client through the entire reimprinting process with another memory. The goal is to have the client get to a point where she cannot find any other instances. This doesn't mean you have reimprinted every memory associated with the issue. It means that the client's unconscious mind has realized the pattern and has generalized the resources out to all of the other times and places associated with the issue. Remember how the Romans conquered the Western world.

In the next five chapters, you will have the chance to explore the key steps of reimprinting at a more in-depth manner.

Chapter 7
Association and Memory Access

Association

The first step of any change process, including reimprinting, involves inviting the client to associate into the problem state. It is important for the neural network that contains the negative state, behavior, and memory to activate so that we, as coaches, can see the state and know how the client looks *in* the problem and *out* of the problem, a key part of calibration. We can also discover how the client is constructing the problem. Finally, the problem network must be active enough that resources can be linked to it.

When the problem state is active, the client will have access to all of the other times and places he has experienced this issue. Remember the principle of state dependent learning. When someone is happy, it becomes very difficult for him to access memories of being sad unless prompted by something or someone else. In which case, his state will change as she accesses those memories. Likewise, when a client is not feeling the problem state, it becomes more difficult for him to access memories of the problem because those neural networks are inactive at the moment. This type of coaching is state based. If the state isn't visible, it becomes more challenging to help him create the change he wants.

Levels of Association

In the world of coaching and hypnosis, we may encounter three levels of association when working with memories:

1. *Hypernesia*
2. *Revivification*
3. *Regression*

The distinction among the three levels is how much of the client's current experience is taken up by the memory, how much of his conscious bandwidth he is using to recall the event.

Hypernesia

At this level, the client talks about the event and can recall specific details but does not have a kinesthetic response to the event. *For example*: You could recall a recent vacation and bring it to mind enough to recall what you did. And you could zoom into the event enough to remember more refined details, such as the time of day and order of events. In this example, the chances are you will not have an emotional or physiological response to the memory beyond knowing that you enjoyed it.

Revivification

To revivify means "to bring back to life." When a memory is revivified, we can feel the emotions connected to it and as if we have stepped back into the event. Part of us experiences the memory while another part is still tracking to some extent the fact that it is a memory.

For example: You could call to mind that vacation again and choose one particularly enjoyable moment. Take your time and really revel in the experience. As you step into that vacation, notice if it's daytime or nighttime; if you're alone or with others; what the ground feels like under your feet; what the temperature is. You could pay attention to how it feels to really enjoy this moment.

In this example, you may have noticed that the experience came more to life for you. If you began to embody the memory—meaning you felt some of the emotions you felt at the time—or you could feel the physical sensations associated with the memory, you are well on your way to revivifying the event.

Regression

Up to this point, I have been using *regression* to refer to reimprinting or in regards to clients who spontaneously enter a regressed state. This use is related to the process; however, this time I am using it to describe the level to which we, as practitioners, help our clients to associate into memories.

Regression takes revivification to its furthest extent. When regressed, the individual is so deeply enmeshed in the memory that he loses touch with his current age. He may step so deeply into the event that he loses touch with his current surroundings and relives the experience as if it were happening in the current moment.

For example: You step into the memory of that pleasant vacation so much so that you forget that you were reading these words and become deeply absorbed in that moment. This means that you would not be focusing on anything that happens after that moment because it hasn't happened yet. The memory becomes the present moment. Of course, you are here and now reading these words knowing that the memory is in the past.

For reconsolidation to occur, revivification is needed as a part of the reimprinting process. Pure regression, however, is not. I suggest that it is useful to think of these levels as being conceptual and not necessarily objectively true. There are no objective ways of measuring them. It will come down to your calibration skills and judgment as a coach. When doing reimprinting, the memory needs to be alive enough for the client to embody it, but it does not need to be a full regression. As long as your client's states are big enough for you to easily see, you are in the right place to help her make lasting positive change.

Helping Your Client to Associate

In the following subsections, you will find four tools to help you associate a client into the problem state. In practice, you will likely use a combination of these tools. These same skills will also be used at other points within the reimprinting.

1. *Be specific*
2. *Use present tense language*
3. *Use echoing*
4. *Use questioning*
5. *Pay attention to the body*

Be Specific

An easy way to help the client associate into a state is to invite him to talk about a specific time and place when he experienced the problem. This will help the neural network associated with the problem to light up, and it will give you a lot more information about how the client is specifically doing the problem. If you are familiar with the strategies of John Overdurf's Coaching Pattern, this is where you will find the moment of *synesthesia* either within or surrounding the memory. This is the moment where the client switches from everything being OK to the problem. When doing reimprinting, this gives us a tremendous wealth of extra information, including what specifically caused the negative emotion in the memory so that, as practitioners, we can add different resources and techniques as needed to the memory and throughout the session.

When asked to speak about a specific time and place, clients often answer with, "It happens all of the time." This occurs because they are used to running an unconscious pattern wherein they have generalized the issue across their life. Their brain is sorting for all instances of the problem, and a natural blind spot develops for all of the moments in daily life when the problem is not there.

There are two methods of overcoming this issue. The first is gentle while the second is playful. The first option is to pace and lead the client by first acknowledging that you understand that it has been going on for a long time and often feels as though it happens all of the time. Then invite the client to tell you about the last time she experienced the issue.

This interaction may look as follows:

> Coach: So tell me about a specific time when you experienced this issue.
>
> Client: It happens all of the time.
>
> Coach: I know you have had this issue for quite a while, and probably tried a number of ways to overcome it, and it does seem like it happens all of the time. How about we start with just talking about the last time you had this issue?

The second way of handling the client's generalization is to become a little playful with her. Indirectly pace her statement and then pose a challenge to her.

It may look as follows:

> Coach: Tell me about a specific time you had this issue.
>
> Client: It happens all of the time.
>
> Coach: Really? Is must be happening right now then?
>
> Client: No, not now but at other times.
>
> Coach: Great, that means you have lots of options. Choose one specific time.

The indirect pace occurs in the fact that you have momentarily taken on your client's belief that it happens all of the time. Logic then dictates that the client must be experiencing it now even though you know she is not. You are indirectly asking the unconscious mind to distinguish between problem and not problem by comparing now to all other times. Once the client is able to distinguish that and recognize it isn't happening now, it becomes much easier for her to find a specific time when the problem was present. The trick with this approach is that you must be in rapport with the client; otherwise, it can come off as a challenge.

Use Present Tense Language

As you begin to speak with your client about that specific instance, it will be useful to shift your language from past tense to present tense. This helps to stabilize the client's experience. Continuing to speak about the instance as though it happened in the past may keep a client dissociated, as he is able to compartmentalize it into something that is over.

To experience the power of language, join me for a short thought experiment. Take a moment and close your eyes. With your eyes closed say to yourself, "I was on a warm beach." Notice what you experience and then open your eyes. Now, for the second round, close your eyes and say to yourself, "I am on a warm beach." Notice what happens this time.

You may have noticed some interesting changes. For some people, more representational systems become involved with the second statement. For others, one or two rep systems become more involved, such as the visual and kinesthetic.

It is important to pace and lead your client with the language tense. To begin in the present tense about something that happened in the past may be a bit jarring for both you and your client and could pull the client out of the moment. Begin by pacing the current experience by referring to the event as being in the past. Set your intention to switch tenses when it feels natural. There is no right or wrong time to do this. At first, you may choose a very specific point in time to switch tenses. As you have more experience with this type of pacing and leading, the tense shift will happen naturally and unconsciously.

Below is an example of tense shifting as a pace and lead.

> Coach: Tell me about the last time and place you experienced this issue.

> Client: It happened two days ago when I was out with my friends.

> Coach: What happened while you were with your friends?
> Client: We were out having fun, and then something caught my eye and I felt afraid.

> Coach: So you're there with your friends and you're having a good time. Where *are* you when this is happening?

Pay close attention to whether the client follows you or not when you make the tense switch. Some clients shift and speak in the present tense as well. This will let you know that they, at some level, have begun the process of associating into the event and subsequent state. Other clients continue to speak in the past tense as if they did not register the tense change in your questioning. If this occurs, you can return to past tense language for a few moments and then transition to present tense and listen if they follow. Some clients fully associate into an experience but never change their language tense to the present. If that is the case, that is perfectly fine to the extent that you can see that they are experiencing the state associated with the memory.

Use Echoing

Words are anchors for individuals. The words that your client uses are selected by the unconscious because they have particular meanings for your client. You can use those anchors to help the client further associate into the experience. Do this by using the same words your client uses. Note that this is not active listening. You do not feed back an approximation of what the client has said; instead, you use the client's precise wording. This is done conversationally so that it seems to the client as though you are simply trying to get more information.

Example:

> Client: I was out with my friends, and I was hoping the dog wouldn't be there, but there he was, and I freaked out.
>
> Coach So you are there with your friends and you are hoping the dog isn't going to be there but there he is... .

The secret to doing this effectively is to not sound as though you are parroting every word the client says. Use this technique sparingly. It feels most natural when stated using a tonality that sounds as though you're repeating back simply for clarification or to set the scene or a tonality of fascination. Remember, the goal is to keep this as conversational as possible.

You don't want an interaction that looks like this:

> Client: I was out with my friends.
>
> Coach: You're out with your friends.
>
> Client: I was hoping the dog wouldn't be there.
>
> Coach: You're hoping the dog wouldn't be there.
>
> Client: I'm trying to act relaxed.
>
> Coach: You're trying to act relaxed.

In this example, the coach interjected too frequently and broke the flow of the client's thoughts. Remember that the objective is to help stabilize the client's experience, not interrupt it.

Use Questioning

You can also help a client to associate into an experience through the types of questions you ask. We explore here two types of questions: binary and sensory-based questions.

Binary-choice questions limit the options and force the unconscious mind to make a distinction. The structure of these questions is very simple: you provide two options from which the client can answer. It's either this or that.

For example: As you associate the client into a specific experience, you could ask her, "Is it daytime or nighttime?" or "Are you alone or with others?" or "Are you inside or outside?" These types of questions conversationally force the client to choose one instance and begin to step into it.

The second type of questioning helps the client associate more deeply into the experience by guiding her to find specific and detailed information about the experience. This type of question focuses specifically on sensory experience.

For example: You could ask the client from which direction is the light coming. Asking about light direction is a powerful means of associating the client because it is not something that humans normally pay a tremendous amount of conscious attention to.

You can also become curious about other aspects of the sensory experience, for example, asking about what is under the client's feet. The feet—the parts of the body furthest from the brain—are more closely linked to unconscious awareness. When the client is able to answer with a response that is appropriate for the memory, she is either fully associated or close to being so.

On rare occasions, some clients, particularly those who live from the neck up, continue to give answers *about* the problem rather than stepping into a specific event. They may do this for a number of reasons. It could be something as simple as their unconscious mind has not yet understood what you are asking the client to do. In these situations, slow down and begin again. You may want to use direct suggestion to help them step into the experience.

Pay Attention to the Body

Finally, you can help your client to associate more completely by becoming curious as to where in the body he is feeling the problem/present state. Bringing conscious awareness to it tends to amplify the emotions. This has the added benefit of indirectly suggesting that the emotion exists in the body and is not reality.

(In later chapters, I speak more about how to utilize the body to help clients associate into states and, more specifically, into resourceful states.)

There may be other instances when the client is not willing to experience the negative state. You can outframe this from the beginning by letting the client know that you are going to ask him to momentarily experience the problem. But it will be short-lived and well worth it. Calibrate whether the unconscious mind agrees before moving forward.

If the client continues to refuse consciously or unconsciously to associate into the state, explore the reasons for that and help the client change that aspect before moving forward. It may also be that the client is not ready or does not want the change. In which case, it would not be effective or ethical to continue.

Finding the Memory

Once the client has associated into the problem state, you can move forward to find the appropriate memory to reimprint. The approach you take will depend on the type of client with whom you're working.

The three different instances where reimprinting is indicated (as described in Chapter 5), each have a unique approach to memory elicitation.

Direct Memory

When a client states that she knows exactly where the issue started, your job is extremely easy. Using the techniques described at the beginning of this chapter, you can fully associate the client into that initial instance. There is no need to associate the client into a recent time or place and then jump back because she already has the pivotal moment in conscious awareness.

The Affect Bridge

There will be some instances in which a client will say that he has had the issue since childhood but cannot consciously pinpoint its starting moment. In this situation, you can leverage the fact that the brain sorts by states. You can use the problem state to find an early memory with which to work.

Remember that memory is plastic. It doesn't matter whether the event actually took place. What matters is that the unconscious mind is using a specific metaphor to explain the existence of the problem. Somewhere in the client's neural networks a connection is creating the metaphor, which we are describing as a memory to explain the issue.

The principle behind the affect bridge is simple: we use the negative state to create memory steppingstones back to the earliest instance where the client experienced the problem. When the client is in the problem state, she will have access to a lot more information related to that problem than when not in that state. This means that when she is in the state, it's much easier to access previous memories, especially when prompted.

Using the affect bridge, we are looking to go back to the earliest instance of this problem. In terms of neuroscience, we are looking to get to the earliest point in the network related to the issue. The further back in time we go, the closer to the base of the neural network we come. We certainly do not need an ISE to change the issue. However, the further down the neural chain you go, the greater the amount of leverage you have in creating the change.

Think about it this way: If you were to change something about your emotional life or personality when you were 7 years old, how much more of a long-term impact would that have had on you now versus having made that same change a week ago. If you made a change at 7 years old, you would have had several years to practice and integrate that change.

There are direct ways of crafting an affect bridge wherein the hypnotist instructs the client to go back in time to find the memory.

The hypnotist may do this by giving direct suggestions:

> As you're feeling that, I'm going to count from three down to one, and when I reach one, you can find yourself in an earlier time when you had that feeling. Three ... two ... one. Be there now.

This approach is perfectly acceptable within the framework of reimprinting. But because this book focuses on a more conversational approach, we are, instead, going to use implication, questions, and instinct to guide the client back through her personal timeline.

When building the affect bridge, the first few memories that come forward tend to be relatively recent in the client's experience. Remember that we are interested in getting as low as possible on the neural chain, so we are not particularly interested in the more recent events at this point.

To help the client move further back in time, we use a simple tag question:

> This isn't the first time you have experienced this, is it?

This question is a fairly safe mind read, especially since the client has already told you that she has had the issue for a long time. The unspoken implication in the above statement suggests that the client brings to mind an earlier time. For the client to agree with your statement, she will have to access an earlier memory. Once she agrees with you, you can then become curious about that earlier instance and urge the client to identify that previous instance.

In the session transcript at the beginning of this book, you will note at first a conversational approach to building the affect bridge.

> Coach: So tell me, James, about the last time and place you experienced this fear.
>
> Client: It was last week. I was at home taking care of my little girl.
>
> Coach: What's happening?
>
> Client: She doesn't feel well, and I'm afraid she might vomit. [The client's physiology shows that he has fully associated into the moment.]
>
> Coach: This is not the first time you have felt this fear, is it?
>
> Client: No.
>
> Coach: What is that earlier instance you are thinking about now?

In this example, the client quickly shifted to present tense language, and his physiology showed the problem state, so there was no need to do more to help him associate. I then conversationally moved him into the earlier time.

This particular client quickly entered trance, so as we continued down the bridge, the need to be conversational diminished. Remember, the more in trance your client is, the less conversational you need to be.

The more direct approach to moving down the bridge may look like this:

> Coach: This is not the first time you have had this feeling either, is it?

> Client: No.

> Coach: Allow the scene to fade and the emotion to take you even further back now. [The coach waits to see the unconscious cue that a memory has been found.] Where are you?

The question then arises, how do you know when to stop bouncing back through time? The first step is to move the client as close to the original event as possible. The client may not know how old she was when the issue started. So, as a coach, it is useful to take her back to memories from the emotional imprinting phase, which ends around 10 years of age, if the bridge goes back that far. Once you are close to the imprinting age, you can be direct and simply ask the client if this is the first time she felt this way. If the client says no, bounce her further back. If she says yes, then you have the first memory to reimprint.

In some instances, you will not want to build an affect bridge. The first is if the client knows exactly where the issue started. The bridge becomes redundant. The other time is when the client has strongly associated into a negative state. Keep in mind that as you build the affect bridge, the emotional state may intensify as you jump back. If you have a client fully associated into a strong negative state, jump her immediately back to the earliest memory.

The easiest way to do this is through direct suggestion:

> Coach: Allow that feeling to take you back to the first time you felt it. Three ... two ... one. Be there now.

Feel comfortable being very direct and taking the lead in these instances. The conversational approach is not needed because the conscious mind's critical factor has already been bypassed.

Embodied Regressions

You have some options when a client shows you a regression in his physiology. The first is to work with the memory that he is currently describing. If the body shows you the physiology of the event, you can certainly begin there, continuing to reimprint a number of problem instances until the change has generalized.

Typically, however, when a client shows you regressed physiology, even if he is speaking about a recent event, the physiology will be linked to when he first learned the issue, sometime in childhood. So why not go where the physiology is pointing? If the client knows where the issue has started, you can you do a one-step affect bridge back to that earlier instance. If he doesn't know, you have a great deal of flexibility in how you approach this.

One way is to do a reimprinting on the current instance. Run through the entire reimprinting process, but instead of using a memory, reimprint the current experience. Do this by inviting the client to step outside of his self (and sometimes change the client's physical location), and then help him to resource the self that is in an unresourceful physiology. Do not associate the client back in until you see the physiology return to that of his adult self. Then from there, you may choose to do more reimprinting work or take a different approach.

Strong Emotional Response

In these instances, the client not only expresses a regressed physiology but also responses that are out of proportion to what is actually happening in the present moment. This is exemplified by the client who comes into your office and instantly enters the problem state without any help from you.

Example: I used to have an office on the 29th floor. It was a fair assumption that clients with a fear of heights or elevators would be showing their emotions by the time they reached my office.

In such cases, you have three options:

1. You can reimprint the present moment so that the client is in a more resourceful place to start.

2. You can reimprint the present moment but assume that the client is caught up in a memory. You can ask how old the client is. When the emotions are strong enough, the client will answer with the age he was in that memory. With this approach, you may invite the client to change positions in your office as he dissociates. Then you will reimprint the memory the client was experiencing.

3. The third option is to help the client dissociate and then move on to a different technique.

I now go into more details about these different approaches. At the heart of this are the same steps laid out in chapter 1. Which of the three categories your client falls within will lead you to select exactly how to do the reimprinting.

Chapter 8
Stepping out of the Memory

Once you have found the memory, it is now useful for you and the client to take a step back. If the client is caught up in the memory, it becomes very difficult to change it, as the client is running a problem trance that most likely will not include you. When the client is completely in the problem state, she will sort only for those things in her experience that are related to the state.

For example: If someone is feeling down, it is very difficult to get her to find times in her life when she is happy. In reimprinting, the client, at one level, is regressed when she associates into the problem. Children are not as powerful as adults are. In that memory, the client is not as resourceful as she is now, so it is important to give her a strategy to step out of, or dissociate from, the memory so she can change it.

There are three main approaches to dissociation that make it easy for the client to return to his current age:

1. *Submodality shifts*
2. *Specific verbal and nonverbal language*
3. *Spatial reorientation*

The Visual Submodalities of Dissociation

Let's begin by trying a thought experiment. Imagine your favorite food, and notice whatever pictures come to mind. Become aware of the size (big, small); its location (in front of you, to the left, to the right, up, down) its brightness (bright, dim); its color (black and white, colored); its motion (still, moving); and its distance (near, far). Now think of a food that you don't like, and notice the different aspects of that picture. Are the qualities of the picture the same as the food you really enjoy, or are they different? You may notice some very interesting differences. (We will return to this later.) For now, let go of the food you don't like, recall the one you enjoy, and then let that go as you move your attention back to the here and now.

The human brain is constantly in search of energy-efficient ways of tracking information. The brain uses up more metabolic energy than any other organ, so it needs ways to conserve that energy. One way it does this is through *submodalities*, the finer distinctions made in our different representational systems. In the above example, you paid attention to some of the distinctions your brain makes in your visual system. Your brain has coded foods you like and those you don't in very specific ways so that every time you think of a food you don't have to waste energy asking yourself if you like it or not or comparing it to other foods. You brain has cut down on the time and energy required by coding those two types of food in different submodalities. If you were to think of any other type of food you like or don't like, you will find that the submodailities are similar to those in this exercise. This extends well beyond foods. You brain does this for everything else you experience as well, and you can use those submodalities to change how you feel and respond.

While submodalities exist in each of the representational systems, for this pattern, we are going to focus on the visual component, in particular distance, size, brightness, location, and association.

Distance, size, and brightness have a strong effect on the emotional impact of images, so changing these goes a long way in helping the client to dissociate, as these are typically driving visual submodalities.

Location is also included to leverage how the client organizes time while association/dissociation is fundamental to this pattern.

Distance

To begin the process of dissociation, invite the client to place the memory "over there on the floor." The memory can be moved to any position that is comfortable to the client. Keep in mind that the closer the memory is to the client, the more difficult it will be for him to dissociate.

Size

As the client moves the memory away, direct the client to make it small. This makes it much harder for the client to be inside of the event, and it provides the client with a different perspective. This will be very useful when it is time to resource the memory.

Brightness

The brightness will typically change as you guide the client to change the distance and size. The submodalities of distance, size, and brightness are linked in our neurology. Things closer tend to be bigger and brighter while things farther away become smaller and dimmer. You may want to give the client suggestions on making it dim if he is still finding it difficult to dissociate.

Location

Slightly less important than the three above submodalities, location is still useful, especially as it can be used as an indirect suggestion. While the client can comfortably work with a memory on the floor in front of her, you can invite the client to place the event down to her left. If the client is normally organized in terms of her timeline, this puts the memory visually in the past. This is a gentle suggestion that the events that she has been running in the client's mind are, in reality, long in the past. If the client organizes time with her future in front of her and the past behind, she will typically unconsciously pick up on the suggestion. When you ask the client who organizes time in this way to put her timeline in front of her so she can see past and future, she will most often put the past to the left. If the client is reversed organized, she certainly will put the event to her right.

In conjunction with moving the memory spatially to the past, suggest that the client place the event on the floor as opposed to keeping it at eye level or anywhere else the client may have been keeping it previously. When it's on the floor, the client gains perspective and is placed in a position of power over the event. The client is more empowered to change her experience of the event.

Association

This is the most obvious of the visual submodalities, as this part of the pattern is all about dissociation. To help the client no longer see the memory through his own eyes (associated), invite him to see his younger self in the image. It is as though he were watching a movie about the event featuring the younger self.

Following is an example of helping a client dissociate through visual submodalities. For the purposes of this example we will call the adult client "Bob."

> Coach: Step outside of that memory now, making it small and putting it on the floor over there. You can make it dim and shrink it to a comfortable size as you are here with me looking at little Bobby over there. That's right. It's small and way over there as you're here with me now looking at the small event over there.

As you help your client make the appropriate submodality changes, be comfortable with being direct. It is your job to anchor the client back in the here and now. You can suggest the changes in submodalities until you see the client's physiology shift into a neutral state.

The Language of Dissociation

How you speak about the memory will influence your client's orientation to the event.

For example: let's do a thought experiment.

Part 1: Imagine a picture of a lemon located to your left. As you glance over there, look at the small picture of that object that was photographed sometime in the past.

Part 2: Now imagine holding this juicy lemon in your hands, feeling the texture. You can cut a fresh slice and bring it up to your mouth and take a bite.

You may have noticed that your experience in part 1 was far more dissociated than it was in part 2. Your clients will have a similar experience, depending on your use of language. To help the clients dissociate fully, utilize the language of space, time, and matter.

Spatial Language

Remember, distance and location are two key submodalities in helping the client dissociate. It's important to keep in mind that while we may give a direct suggestion for the submodality shift, we need to maintain that change throughout a large part of the pattern. The easiest way to use spatial language is to refer to the memory as being "over there" or "down there" and the client as being "here" or "up here." The use of "there" for the memory and "here" for the client keeps the client in the space with you and not lost in the memory. Of course, you can use any other spatial adverbs or prepositions to maintain the separation of the client from the memory. The use of "here" and "there" is an easy and effective way of delineating between the client and the memory.

Temporal Language

This is fairly obvious but worth a reminder. Any time you refer to the events in the memory before you do the reimprinting, use past tense language. (In the next chapter, you will gain a good understanding of how and when to bounce between past and present tense language. However, in the initial dissociation phase, use past tense verbs, and refer to events as being in the past.)

Names

Using the client's name within the context of the memory is another simple and powerful way to use language to help the client dissociate. This means that when you talk about the events in the memory, you will refer to the client's younger self by the client's first name instead of "you." If the client had a nickname at that time, you can also use that nickname to refer to the younger self in the memory.

Try this thought experiment for moment: Think of a pleasant memory from childhood. Now step out of that memory and watch it play out on the floor as if you were watching yourself in a movie. Now say to yourself, "I am having a good time," and be aware of how that feels. Now say to yourself, "(your name) was having a good time." Notice how your feelings change. You may have noticed that the second time through the feeling diminished. The event is no longer happening to you but is happening to that person in the memory. If you had a nickname as a child that you no longer have, you can do this a third time and say to yourself "(your nickname) was having a great time." Be aware of how you feel this time. You may notice an even larger degree of separation between your current self and that younger version of you in the memory. When using a childhood nickname, it may even feel as though the person in the event is completely separate and different from the current self. Since this was a pleasant memory, you can step back inside and really enjoy it and allow it to fade back to where it came from.

Reorientation

Occasionally, a client may still find it difficult to completely dissociate from the memory. You still see a child-like physiology even though the client believes she is carrying on an adult conversation. When this

72

occurs, you can reorient her to the present moment and change the relationship to the memory by first having her open her eyes, if the eyes were closed. This helps to ground the client in the present moment with you. You can continue the reimprinting by encouraging her to go through the process with her eyes open.

You can also invite her to stand up and move around. The memory can stay where it's placed on the floor while you and the client move to a different location in relationship to that memory, remembering to keep the memory in the client's past spatially.

This has a two-layered benefit. The first is that it encourages the client to change her physiology, which will automatically lead to a state change. On another level, this indirectly suggests to the client's unconscious mind to take on a different perspective in regard to the event being reimprinted. The client may notice new things about the memory that she hadn't considered before that can help her in making this change.

It is very important that the client is properly dissociated from the memory so that she fully engages in the next step of the process, the resourcing of the event. If a client is still stuck in the memory, she is not neurologically as resourceful as she otherwise could be.

If the client does not dissociate enough to at least elicit a neutral state despite your best efforts to help her dissociate, do something different. In extremely rare circumstances, the client becomes so wrapped up in the events that the dissociation process can take quite a long time. I explore this more in a later chapter when I address the issue of abreactions. For now, keep in mind that if it takes a substantial amount of time to dissociate the client, you may want to consider a different approach than reimprinting at this time. You may come back to the reimprinting later; however, it may be more beneficial to the client to engage in some other pattern. This will be up to your judgment in this specific instance.

Once the client is dissociated and can speak with you as an adult about the event in the memory, move on to the next step and the next chapter.

Chapter 9
Reimprinting the Memory

The next two steps of the reimprinting process, the resourcing and gifting, are covered in this chapter. This is because both steps happen a number of times throughout the reimprinting process. At this stage, you will be alternating between associating into strongly positive states and moving those states into the memory.

In terms of neuroscience, the reconsolidation of the memory begins with the steps covered in this chapter and the next.

The Order

As you continue in this process, you will guide your client to resourcing each player in the memory. Begin with the younger version of the client in the memory. Typically, the younger self holds the least amount of power or influence in the event. By resourcing him first, the client unconsciously places himself in a position of power in relationship to the events in the memory.

It is important to remember that you're not changing the content of the memory—although some clients express this changing naturally. The reimprinting changes the emotions contained within the memory as well as those in relationship to the memory. The implication is that if the younger self is more resourceful, the memory, by default, must change and the current version of the client must be more resourceful, which, in turn, makes the rest of the process very easy.

The second group to be resourced is those who are present within the memory. The assumption here is that those in the memory were also not as resourceful as they could have been; otherwise, the events would not have occurred the way they had. As the client begins to resource one person at a time, it becomes very important for you, as coach, to help him reframe the actions of those other individuals. (I speak more about this later in this chapter.) This also changes how the client feels about those individuals in the memory in a more positive way.

The third group to be resourced is anyone who wasn't there and should have been. There are occasions when something occurs in the client's life when perhaps a mother or father or friend should have been there but were not. Resourcing those individuals allows the client to put their absence into context. On the neurological level, it introduces those people into the memory engram that is being reconsolidated.

Even though those individuals were not in the narrative of the memory, they are now brought in as an added resource to the memory. Some clients may actually add those individuals to the story of the memory. They will be aware that the person wasn't, in reality, there. The resources that the person brings add to the positive states being built into the memory.

For example: Think of some difficult moment in your life, and recall how it feels. Now step out of that memory and place it on the floor. If you could introduce someone else into the memory who would make the difference for you now, perhaps a friend, coach, or someone else important to you, who would that be? As you imagine that person, gift to him or her the ability to enter that memory. Now watch what happens when that memory plays out with the newly added person. If you want to, you can even step inside of the memory and experience it with that person there supporting you. Even though, logically, you know the person wasn't present, it still changes the emotions in the memory to have him or her there. This was a simple thought experiment. When you do the reimprinting process, this happens on a very deep level.

Resourcing

At this stage, you help your client to resource those involved in the event (or not) one person at a time. The process, as described in this section and the next section, is done with each individual, or "player," as appropriate for the client. Keep in mind that it is essential that the resource states are more powerful than the negative state originally in the memory. The more powerful the state, the more neural connections it has.

For example: If your client chooses happiness and experiences a strong state of happiness, it is fair to assume that he has countless reference experiences throughout his life of happiness and, consequently, many neural connections for it. This means that there's more neurological leverage on the side of happiness. The state with the more neural connections is going to win out during the reconsolidation process.

The Question to Ask

To begin the resourcing, ask your client one simple yet vital question. Beginning with the younger self, ask the present-age client, "What resources did she need in that situation that would make the difference for you now today?" The structure of this question invites the client to jump between past and present. The question presupposes that as the client goes through the steps, she will, in fact, change now. It catches the client in a double bind because by naming and experiencing the resource, she must change.

Feel free to use of the following questions or any variation there of:

- If (younger self name) could be any way different that would make all of the difference for you now, how would she be?

- What skills could (younger self) use that would make the

77

difference for you today?

- If (younger self) could feel any way different in that situation that would make the difference for you now, how would she feel?

Associate into the Resource State

The client will typically name one state at a time. Beginning with the first state, guide the client to fully associating into that emotion. There are a number of methods of association. You can use the same techniques detailed earlier in this book. But instead of using it for the problem state, you can use it for the resource. A nice addition is to help the client get in touch with the sensation of the positive emotion in her body. You can explore the submodalities of that feeling as well and become curious about its color.

Example:

"Coach: If she could be any way different in that situation that would make the difference for you now, how should she be?

Client: She would be calm.

Coach: That's right. And you know what it's like to be calm, don't you? [Waits for the unconscious head nod.] And what is it like when you are really calm?

Client: I just relax and feel at peace in my body and mind.

Coach: And as you're beginning to feel that now, where does it start in your body?

Client: In my breathing.

Coach: And where does it move to next?

Client: It moves through my shoulders and through the rest of me.

Coach: And I'm curious; does that feeling of calmness have a color?

Client: Yes, it's blue.

Coach: That's right, and just enjoy that blue as it continues to develop and you can really feel that sense of calm." [The coach calibrates to see the client fully associate into a sense of calmness as indicated by the physiology.]

Gifting

Once you see the strong positive state in your client's physiology, invite him to gift it to the player in the memory in any way appropriate. Some players might like to send the emotional energy of a positive state into the memory. Others send the color of the emotion or a symbol of the emotion into the memory. Still others choose to speak with the players in the memory as a means of resourcing them. Whichever way makes most sense to your client is the ideal way.

After a player is gifted, invite your client to watch the memory replay and notice how it is different. Typically, the client responds positively. The client gives a positive verbal description, meaning that the memory might be more calm or distant. While those words serve as anchors for the client, also calibrate to the client's physiology and checking to see if he is still in a resourceful state when the changed memory is described.

Reconsolidation

After each player has been resourced, you can give the client the option of stepping into the new memory and feel from the inside out how it is different. Some clients choose to step inside while others opt not to. In some circumstances, it is not appropriate for the client to step back into the movie, for example, in the case of abuse. Other than that, if a client is reluctant to step into the memory, there might be some more work to do. Use your best judgment as you calibrate to the changes in the client's physiology.

Once the client steps into the memory this time, run him through the memory and grow him up into his current age. This step integrates the new interpretation of the memory into other neural networks and gives the client a sense of who he is as a complete person. It is important to initiate the growing up from the specific memory you have just altered, as it will place the memory in the appropriate context, time, and place on the client's timeline. This also has the hidden benefit of reimprinting unconsciously other subsequent events. Because the client has had the experience of changing this memory, who knows just how many other things can change in a positive direction?

Chapter 10
Forgiveness

A long time ago two Buddhist monks were on a pilgrimage. The first monk was a young student, new to the order. The second monk was his teacher. One day as they were walking along the river, they came across an elderly woman desperately trying to cross the water. With no boats available, the senior monk picked the woman up and carried her on his back across to the other side. Even though this action was taboo to the particular order the monks belonged to, the elder monk did not hesitate to help. When they reached the other side, the elder monk placed the old woman on the shore and they bade each other farewell. As the two monks continued on their journey the younger monk became increasingly agitated as he turned over the events of the day in his head.

Eventually the young monk couldn't take it anymore and he stopped his teacher and said, "I can no longer study with you, Master."

The senior monk was perplexed and asked why.

The younger monk said, "I can no longer consider you a teacher because you have broken the vows of our order by touching a woman."

The senior monk smiled at his student as he said, "I put the woman down hours ago on the other side of the river, and yet you have been the one who has been carrying her this entire time. Who has really broken the vows?"

While on the surface the story is very clever, there's also a deep insight for us and our clients. When clients have memories that need reimprinting, they very often carry negative feelings and associations with the people involved in the event alongside those memories. Even if the memory is reimprinted, if the client still holds a negative emotion towards any of the players, it could possibly undo the change.

Parts

We can conceptualize the problematic memory as being a neural network within the larger neural system of our clients. Up until they've come to see us for hypnosis, the clients have spent a lot of time consciously bouncing around within the neural network, within the memory, trying to change it from the inside out. As they've done this, they have inadvertently strengthened the neural connections that create the negative state in the memory. They have kept the memory alive in such a way that they've built robust negative neural connections around it.

Through the reimprinting process, we've attached a much larger, more resourceful state to the memory cutting away the negative emotional response. The question then becomes: What happens to the old connections, the negative associations once the memory has been reprinted?

Over the next several weeks the clients' brain go through a process known as *neural pruning* where inactive pathways are repurposed for something more useful. For this to take place, we need to ensure that the clients don't refire the old negative pathways. One very useful way of doing this is to dissolve any boundaries between the memory network and the rest of the clients' neurological system. This is easily achieved through forgiveness.

Numerous studies have shown the positive emotional impact of forgiveness and how it alters brain activity. One study showed specifically how forgiveness activates not only the empathy centers of the brain but also the hippocampus, which you will remember is in charge of consolidation and reconsolidation. This means that when we introduce forgiveness, our clients not only dissolve the boundaries of the problem network but also go through another round of positive reconsolidation of the event.

What Is Forgiveness?

A lot of clients, and people in general, view forgiveness as forgetting or excusing wrongdoing. Clients may from time to time express this.

Forgiveness, in actuality, is neither about excusing nor forgetting. It is making the active decision to no longer be tied to the event and the actions of others in that memory. Forgiveness is a client's declaration of freedom from the past. It has everything to do with the client and very little to do with anyone else involved. Remember our two monks at the beginning of this chapter. We can introduce forgiveness in a number of ways. The next section shows you how to preframe it for your clients. I then share the technique most often used at the end of every imprinting to create that sense of letting go.

Preframing Forgiveness

As mentioned above, clients may be reluctant at first to consider forgiving those who wrong them in the memory. This creates an interesting quandary. If a client goes through every imprinting and at the end is unwilling to forgive the participants, the coach may become curious as to whether a full reimprinting has taken place. It becomes a chicken or the egg type question. To sidestep this issue, introduce the role of forgiveness before moving into the full reimprinting.

An easy way to do this is using metaphor. You have one example of a typical forgiveness metaphor at the beginning of this chapter. Another metaphor comes from Gandhi. He said, "Anger is like drinking poison and expecting the other person to die." This is a powerful statement when a client stops to really consider its implications.

I have found in my own practice that some of the most powerful metaphors for clients come out of neuroscience. Clients really enjoy learning about the brain and how to use it more efficiently. This type of metaphor is ideal when clients really struggle with the idea of forgiveness, as explaining the research about how forgiveness affects the brain makes the process completely about the client.

If you share these types of metaphors with your client first, and then approach the topic of forgiving the participants, more often than not your clients will be open to the idea even before the reimprinting. As you tell these metaphors, it is essential that you calibrate the clients' unconscious responses. When you talk about forgiveness, in what way does the physiology shift? Do the clients become more or less resourceful?

When to Address Forgiveness

We leave this is up to your own discretion. Typically, I gently approach the subject of forgiveness before going into the full reimprinting. I may inquire as to how the client feels about forgiving the people involved and then calibrate the unconscious response. Is the client congruent with what he's saying verbally and physically? Or is there an incongruence? An incongruence appears when the client believes you want to hear one response but he feels the opposite. So the client may say that he has forgiven those involved, but his physiology shifts into an unresourceful state. If that occurs, this is an area to explore.

If you are going to use the forgiveness piece of the pattern, I recommend that you introduce it and discuss it before beginning the reimprinting, as opposed discussing it after the pattern, that is, just as you are about to do the forgiveness piece. This allows you to calibrate the client's openness ahead of time. If the client unconsciously objects, that indicates there is some more work to do, possibly before starting the reimprinting or during it. Finally, it ensures the client does not feel as though she is being forced into forgiving.

I also suggest always asking the client first, as there may be times when it is not appropriate or the client outright refuses to engage in this part of the process. Metaphors can be a useful way to reframe some of that reluctance, but it is never useful to force something unwanted on a client. (At the end of this chapter, we explore what to do in instances where forgiveness is not an option.)

The Technique

The easiest ways to help the client to forgive those involved is to invite the client to create in her mind a space in which he is in control. Oftentimes this might be a kitchen table. Some people prefer the idea of sitting around a campfire. Others have a special inner sanctuary. It doesn't really matter where the client chooses to go in his mind to the extent that he is comfortable and relaxed and knows that he is in control of what's about to happen.

One by one the client can invite the people involved in the situation into the space. Only one person will appear at a time. The invitee can remain silent as the client speaks to him or her. This is the client's opportunity to say anything that up until now has been left unsaid. This is his chance to get everything off his chest and finally claim emotional freedom. Once he has said everything that needs to be said, the client is now invited to offer forgiveness to that individual. Once that occurs, the individual can disappear in any appropriate way.

There is no particular order for the appearance of individuals. However, at the end of the process, it is useful for the client to invite in his younger self from that situation. This gives the client the opportunity to forgive himself, thereby diminishing the opportunity for any meta-issues to emerge. It is useful, at this moment, to offer the client some reframes around the younger self making the best decision available and acting with the client's best interest at heart. At this point, the self can merge with the adult and grow up through the years to the present age.

Example:

Coach: Isn't it comforting to know that you can make changes like this easily and quickly? Now we can help to solidify the change even further by just closing your eyes for a moment and imagining you're in a place that makes your feel safe and calm. It could be somewhere you know in your daily life or somewhere your mind creates. Either way is better because you are going to use this space to make lasting change on a deep level. It may be a weird thing to think about, but there were people in your past who were doing the best they could but may have helped to maintain those old emotions. For example: Your mom did the best she could, yet there may be things that you would like to say to her in this space as you forgive anything that needs forgiving and you fully let go of that old issue. So take a moment and invite your mom into this space, saying whatever you need to say to her in order for you to move forward. ... That's right. Now, there may be someone else, such as your aunt. You can invite her in and say what needs to be said as you forgive her and let go. You may consciously think there is no forgiveness needed, and you would be right to rest assured knowing that this is an important step for you. ... Very good. As she leaves this space, is there anyone else who needs to be forgiven for having any involvement with that old issue?

Client: Yes, the kids at school.

Coach: So invite them in one at a time and say whatever needs to be spoken for you to fully enjoy your new freedom. ... That's it. Is there anyone else?

Client: No.

Coach: Might I suggest one more person, the most

important person?

Client: [Nods head.]

Coach: Little Jimmy. He did the best he could throughout your life to keep you safe and happy. He was so loving as a small boy that he reacted the only way he knew how in that moment. Invite him in and thank him for everything he did for you. Let him know what a good job he did. ... That's right. ... Take all of the time you need to do this. When you're ready, give him a hug. Let him melt into you, become a part of you.

As a change-worker you will recognize the individuals that the client is forgiving as in actuality a part of himself. The client has been carrying around mental representations of those involved in the event along with emotions about them and the event, but these are not separate from the client. These internal representations are parts of the network associated with the memory. By forgiving the individuals involved, the client is, in actuality, freeing up those parts of the neural network.

When Forgiveness Is Not Appropriate

That being said, there are specific times and places where it may not be appropriate to address forgiveness. These instances include times when the client's unconscious mind refuses to engage in forgiveness and in instances where the trauma was so severe that the client is not yet ready to forgive. This second category may include instances of rape and abuse. The key here is to calibrate. Allow the unconscious mind to set the pace. There is no need to force someone into forgiveness who is genuinely not ready, no matter how beneficial we may believe it to be as coaches. Over time, the client may change her mind.

In these situations, lead the client through a different type of integration where forgiveness is not introduced. The client can still create a safe place in her mind and use it as an opportunity to communicate to those involved in anything that needs to be said while the other person remains completely silent and unable to respond. The benefit of running this pattern is that it allows the client to burn out a significant proportion of emotional energy surrounding the individuals in the event. The client may find, later on, that she is, in fact, ready to forgive, in which case you can facilitate this experience again.

While forgiveness is not an essential part of the conversational reimprinting, it is a powerful tool in helping clients to let go of the past and rewire their brains in new and resourceful ways. Many clients find this portion of the process to be the moment of personal transformation. The benefit as well is that it places the client in a true position of power in respect to the others involved. In the previous chapter, we saw how the gifting of resources to others contributes to this, and now the client is placed in the position of either bestowing or refusing forgiveness.

In the next chapter, we explore instances where either the reimprinting or parts of the reprinting process may not be appropriate and what to do in those situations.

Chapter 11
Contraindications

As with any piece of change work, it is vital to use common sense with this pattern. Of the three instances when a reimprinting is indicated, the client automatically regresses, her emotional response is incongruent with the situation, or she states she knows where the issue started. The first instance requires some sort of immediate intervention, whether you choose to do a full reimprinting or to bring the client back to the present moment and do something else. The second response may not need to be immediately addressed. In the third instance, where a client knows where the issue comes from, it is important to stop and consider how appropriate it is to work directly with that memory or even to build an affect bridge and jump the client into that experience.

Following you will find the instances where regression work may be contraindicated. As always, use your best judgment as the coach/hypnotist.

Instances of Violence

As mentioned elsewhere in instances of extreme trauma, abuse, and violence, it may not be appropriate to use a reimprinting as the first step in the process or at any point in the client's healing journey. A number of other areas may need to be explored first before the client is ready to take this step. In those situations as well, it is vital that you use extreme care and keep the client as dissociated as possible.

Abreactions

There is a lot of confusion on the topic of abreactions within the hypnosis community. In my view of the world, tears and the experience of emotions are not abreactions. Tears can be a very useful part of the process for healing. One metaphor that I like to use with clients who do experience crying is that we have two different types of tears. The first type of tear keeps the eyes moist and is cried as tears of joy. The chemical components of these tears are very close to saline. The second type of tear helps to clear away emotions and toxins from the body. The chemical structure of this tear is very different and has been shown to remove impurities. So tears are an opportunity for the body and mind to cleanse and heal.

An abreaction, on the other hand, is such an intense emotion that a client fully associates into the memory to the extent that she loses track of the outside world, acts irrationally, and is unable to pull herself out of the experience. A true abreaction is extremely rare within the one-on-one coaching experience. The likelihood of the average practitioner seeing one is infinitesimally small. With that said, it is useful to identify it should it appear and know how to handle it in a way that helps your client.

Step 1: Stay Grounded

This first step for handling abreaction has to do with you as the coach or hypnotist. It is vital that you stay grounded in the present moment. This means that you maintain the frame that there is nothing your client can express or experience within the session that you cannot help him through. Your job is to stay present in the moment and not get pulled into the client's drama. The natural response for most people when they see an abreaction is to become highly concerned, so much so that the practitioner herself panics. If both the client and the practitioner are down the rabbit hole of emotions, who will be there to help pull you both out? Remember that you are a highly skilled coach and know that your client is infinitely resourceful, which means he just needs the right guidance to access those resources and pull himself out of the negative state.

Step 2: Do Not Touch

Different hypnotists have varying views as to whether to touch the client within sessions. Regardless of your personal view, within the context of an abreaction, do not touch the client. The reason for this is very simple: you risk anchoring that touch with the negative state. This is another instance where we have to fight our natural human instinct to reach out and physically comfort someone in pain. The problem is that either you or the actual touch becomes anchored to the state, which could be fired off again later in very inappropriate contexts. So until she is back in the here and now, refrain from touching or hugging the client.

Step 3: Dissociate

In previous chapters, you learned many techniques to help your clients to dissociate from memories; the same techniques can be used here. Use direct suggestion, along with submodality shifts and a change in physical location, to help bring your client back to the here and now.

If you know other change modalities, such as Emotional Freedom Technique (EFT), this can be a wonderful tool to help your client dissociate from the event and reassociate into the present moment. It's very important no matter what techniques you employ here that they draw the client back to the present moment. In this moment, you are the client's only contact with the present, which means you need to be very direct. Think of the abreaction as a very deep trance, which means the client will be open to your suggestions.

Step 4: Wrap It Up

Once the client is back in the present moment, feel free to bring some humor in. Anything to get your client smiling and laughing will be very useful. This is not the time to talk about the abreaction or the events in the memory. You don't want to run the risk of revivifying the abreaction. The best way to segue is to simply acknowledge that the client just had a big experience and then move her attention elsewhere. Do not ask for details of what had happened or try to explore any further in the session.

If something like this were to occur in a session, you can see it as the client's unconscious mind telling you exactly where the issue is and where the change needs to occur. However, you may need to take it very slow and utilize a number of techniques. More dissociated techniques, such as a Change Personal History Pattern, might be useful in the circumstances.

Abreactions are very rare. They are typically a spontaneous and organic regression. Depending on the client and your relationship with him, if he dissociates enough from the emotions, you could attempt the reimprinting. However, in most cases, it's much more useful to bring the client back fully to the here now and to move on to something else. This will be at your discretion based on what you know about the client and your previous coaching history with him.

Chapter 12
Unconscious Reimprinting

Throughout the rest of the book, I will present a number of variations on reimprinting. This chapter focuses on how you can directly leverage unconscious processing to lead the reimprinting.

All reimprinting relies on unconscious involvement, and trance will be present regardless of the presence of a formal induction or not. There are also certain times when it is useful to rely solely on the unconscious mind to reimprint the events. In this chapter, I present a deep-trance form of reimprinting that relies fully on the unconscious mind to make the necessary changes.

Why?

Unconscious reprinting puts complete trust in the unconscious mind of the client to create the desired change. It is a useful strategy in instances where either memories are not available or the client does not want to explore the memories helping to create the negative state and behavior. Unconscious reprinting allows you to work completely on a metaphoric level and a deep-trance level. There are also specific times in which an unconscious reimprinting is indicated.

Anytime a reimprinting is indicated, you can take the unconscious route. There are also some key times when it is more beneficial to use a more unconscious approach. The first is if a client knows the issue comes from the past but can't access any memories connected with the state even after building an affect bridge. In these instances, respect the unconscious mind's desire to keep the memories associated with the problem state out of conscious awareness.

The next instance is when a client spontaneously regresses yet does not have access to the information related to the regression. On occasion, a client may drop into regressed emotions and behaviors. But even once dissociated there is no content that can be reimprinted, at least consciously.

Unconscious reprinting works well in conjunction with other hypnotic processes. It gives you flexibility to do a reimprinting at any point in the session without the need to bring the client's conscious mind into awareness of the processes taking place. With most therapeutic clients, at some point in the process, I typically use an unconscious reimprinting to clean up any instances in the past that we have not worked with, were outside the client's awareness, or were previous reference experiences for the problem. Some clients use previous experiences of having the problem as a confirmation of the problem existing. They can use those past experiences as a way of undermining therapeutic progress by looking back at those previous events and using them to create a belief that the problem still exists.

An example of this is a client who was afraid of flying in the past. The client goes through a change process in which he moves forward but calls to mind all of the instances before coaching where he was afraid. He then uses those instances to create fear again in the present moment. Unconscious reprinting gives the unconscious mind the space needed to let go of the emotions surrounding these old memories and reintegrate them into the whole system in a more resourceful way.

The Technique

You can use this technique for one specific memory, whether consciously known or not, or for multiple memories. I typically use some version of this as a part of the therapeutic process for many clients. This is particularly useful for clients who are gifted at going into deep trances and who have a positive regard for their unconscious minds.

This is ideally done once the client has had a number of reference experiences of generating her own resourceful states. Those previous experiences will have primed the conscious and unconscious mind for the experience the client is about to have.

This pattern leverages arm levitation as the primary external indicator of completion of the process. It also draws on the idea of positive intentions, as it is often used in a six-step reframe.

Step 1: Arm Levitation

This reimprinting begins by suggesting to the client, already deeply in trance, that there may have been other instances in the past that contributed to the experience of the problem state or behaviors that haven't been addressed yet. Calibrate your client for an unconscious head nod or any other indicator of unconscious agreement. Once received, continue. If there is a clear unconscious "no" signal, move on to another part of your process with the client.

Suggest that the client's unconscious mind go through and find those other instances from the past that, when changed, will make the difference for her. The unconscious mind can choose to keep those memories outside of conscious awareness or bring them into conscious awareness. In this pattern, we are not particularly interested in the details of the events. This is also different from other reimprintings because we invite the unconscious mind to find multiple instances at one time as opposed to working with one instance at a time. As the unconscious mind finds those memories, the arm can begin to lift.

Arm levitation causes a lot of new hypnotists more anxiety than needed. All clients are capable of achieving this simple hypnotic phenomenon—although some clients may need a bit more training than others. If you give the direct suggestion, the arm will lift as the unconscious mind performs this task. Pay attention to the quality of the movement of the arm. If it is slow and jerky, you know that it is the unconscious mind lifting the hand. If it lifts quickly and smoothly, this is conscious interference, in which case you can slow the process down.

For naïve clients who have no experience with arm levitation, give a number of reference experiences before doing this pattern. You can invite the client to consciously lift her hand as slowly as humanly possible. Have her fully focus on lifting the hand 1 cm. at a time. This is a very difficult task for the conscious mind to do over a long period; eventually the unconscious mind will take control of the hand. Another technique is to invite the client to consciously lift the hand an inch off her lap and then invite the unconscious mind to lift it another inch. Continue to balance between conscious and unconscious movement each time spending more time in the unconscious movement.

You can also use metaphors or simply lift the arm. Use ambiguous touch and induce catalepsy. Then give the suggestions for the raising and lowering of the arm. Whichever way you choose to teach your client this hypnotic skill, be sure to supply a number of positive hypnotic suggestions about how useful this is for the client and how easily she can experience it other times with you.

Assuming that you have arm levitation, suggest the unconscious mind to find all of those instances in the past as the arm lifts. Once the unconscious mind has found those instances, the arm can stop. Suggest the arm stay where it is.

Step 2: Positive Intentions

Behind everything that we do and feel is a positive intention. We humans are programmed genetically for success; therefore, we are designed to act in ways that we believe will lead us to the greatest amount of success. That doesn't mean that everything we do is inherently resourceful. We make the best choices available to us at the time based on circumstances or filters. Behaviors or feelings identified as "problems" have an unconscious positive intent underneath. The unconscious mind behaves in a problematic way because it believes that this "problematic" behavior is the best choice or that the behavior is providing something truly good for the client.

For example: A smoker smokes because he believes it helps him to relax. Someone else may feel anxiety because on a deep level the unconscious mind is interested in establishing safety.

With the client's arm resting in the air, begin to reframe those memories by speaking with the unconscious mind about the positive intentions behind those states, behaviors, and events. The unconscious mind has selected those memories because there is something of value in them for the client at the present moment.

Suggest the unconscious mind go through those memories and find the positive intention and important message behind those memories.

The arm will lift and stop only once the positive intention or those positive intentions and lessons have been uncovered. The unconscious mind may choose to let the conscious mind in on the secret, in which case, the client can feel free to share it with you if useful. Other times the client will not know consciously.

You may want to provide the unconscious mind with some possible suggestions of what those intentions could be. This acts to directionalize the search and not necessarily to impose any particular positive intention.

The easiest way to do this is to suggest something like this:

> Some unconscious minds are interested in safety while others, happiness. Some unconscious minds are creating wholeness while others, something else completely.

It is not important what words you fill in as long as they are values. Values are words that make people feel good.

Step 3: Resourcing

Once the positive intentions have been found and the arm has stopped lifting, apply those resources back into the memory. The idea here is that if there is a positive intention that the unconscious mind is trying to meet within a problematic state or behavior, it is doing so because that particular value is missing at that time. If you recall the smoker, when he is relaxed, the desire for relaxation is no longer driving the compulsion to smoke.

Invite the unconscious mind to fully step into those positive intentions and feel what it's like to have them completely. Remind the client that he has had a number of experiences stepping into those resources during the coaching process. Calibrate the client and look for a positive-state change as reflected in his physiology.

When you can see the state change, you can continue. Suggest that the unconscious mind place those good feelings into each of those memories. As the unconscious mind does this, the arm can lower. The client will know the process is complete when the hand reaches his lap.

Throughout this pattern, the arm levitation is an indicator for both you and the client as to where the unconscious mind is in the process. This also serves as a strong convincer for the client's conscious mind that the unconscious mind is doing something very important. For some clients, this will be the first time that they've had the experience of their unconscious mind acting outside of conscious control, yet they can be consciously aware of it. This inadvertently creates a conscious–unconscious dissociation, which can be another powerful hypnotic tool for the change process. Although beyond the scope of this book, if you are interested in integrating the conscious–unconscious dissociation, build up the client's curiosity as well as her "not knowing" around the experience, and use that to imply that the unconscious mind can do many important things outside of conscious awareness, including the experience the client is having now.

Chapter 13
Ericksonian Regressions

There is little doubt about the contributions of Milton Erickson to hypnosis and his innovative approaches to family therapy and psychotherapy, including the use of regression work. Unlike his Freudian predecessors, Erickson neither saw the unconscious mind as a dark, scary place nor viewed regression as requiring the patient to relive trauma to gain insights and eventual catharsis. Erickson took a very difference stance. Because the unconscious is a treasure trove of resources, his patients could go back in time to find the resources they needed to make changes in the present moment.

While Erickson never shied away from direct suggestion, and certainly used it in the legendary *February Man*, he did the bulk of his regression work indirectly and in a way that drew out the client's natural resourcefulness. For Erickson, children are inherently resourceful. They are naturally inquisitive, open, and able to quickly learn. Helping clients get back in touch with their child-self calls on those same resources, which will aid in the change process.

Erickson's Therapy

Before diving into the regression technique, it is useful to consider how Milton Erickson saw the therapeutic process.

One of his most significant contributions to hypnosis and family therapy was beyond language patterns and hypnotic techniques: it was Erickson's view of clients, their problems, and their solutions. Clients do not come to therapy or hypnosis because they need to be fixed. Needing to be fixed implies two dangerous ideas.

The first is that clients are in some way broken. Erickson came from a medical background and was educated to see patients as sick or healthy. If they were sick, they go to the doctor to get cured. They certainly don't go the doctor to learn and evolve as a person. He took a very different view from others in the medical community. People do not come to therapy to be fixed or cured. They come to learn and strengthen the rapport with their own unconscious mind.

The second implication is that the therapist knows better than the client what the client's experience of the problem is and what the client needs to be cured of. While it could be argued that Erickson did not completely break away from this belief, he did hold such a deep respect for the client's unconscious mind that he created a space wherein that client could grow.

In this model of hypnosis, clients do not need to be fixed. They need to learn, move past limitations, and create a stronger relationship with their own unconscious mind. Hypnosis creates the appropriate atmosphere in which the client can learn. For Erickson, learning is the central metaphor and resource for client transformation.

Erickson had such a profound trust in the unconscious mind and the client's ability to make lasting change that he often set the scene with an Early Learning Set and then allowed the unconscious to take the learnings that were needed at that time without the hypnotist's interference.

The Early Learning Set

Erickson's primary strategy for helping clients step into their younger selves was the Early Learning Set. This technique uses universal childhood experiences to entice the client to go back in time. On a neurological level, this approach leverages neurological scaffolds. This is the inner framework for understanding ourselves and reality that is built during childhood. When you tap into a scaffold, you access some of the most powerful neural networks in a client and, consequently, have a lot of neurological power behind the change processes you will be doing with the client.

The Early Learning Set is an indirect regression. Clients, in most cases, will not recognize this as a regression.

Erickson used this technique both as therapeutic process and a way to format the unconscious. As a therapeutic process, it is useful in helping clients move beyond unresourceful beliefs, expand beyond self-imposed limitations, or tap into a childhood quality that would be useful now. When formatting the unconscious, the Early Learning Set was often used as a part of the hypnotic induction. The metaphor here was usually around learning new things with a sense of curiosity and achievement. The implication was that the client would carry the curiosity throughout the therapeutic process and into the outside world where she would experience many achievements.

The Process

Step 1: Universal Experience

Choose an experience that your client was likely to have had growing up. Something during the imprint stage is ideal. There is no need to ask your client because even if he didn't experience it, or in the way that you talk about it, he will still draw meaning out of the metaphor.

Common Experiences

- Learning to read and write
- Learning mathematics
- Learning to ride a bike
- Learning to tie a shoe
- Learning to walk

Choosing which experience—whether one listed here or one of your own— will depend on the particular client, his interests, and the reasons he is coming to see you.

For example: Someone who needs more resilience may benefit from the "learning to ride a bike" loop. When a child first learns to ride a bike, she usually has a parent holding the bike steady or perhaps has training wheels to stabilize her balance. Eventually, though, the training wheels come off and the parent lets go of the bike. The child learns how to balance, steer, and pedal all at the same time. At some point, however, it's bound to happen—the child falls. She is determined though and gets up, dusts herself off, and tries again. She goes through a series of falls and getting back up as she learns to adjust to balancing and moving at the same time.

This metaphor taps into a deeply ingrained experience for the client and suggestions that she be resilient now and into the future just as she was when she learned to ride a bike.

I encourage you not to pick something that you know was not a completely positive experience. *For example*: Someone with dyslexia who was teased in school will probably not enjoy being taken back in time to when she learned to read and write.

Step 2: Moving from General to Specific

The set begins with a preframe around children and their ability to learn. There is nothing specific to the client in this moment. After the preframe, the idea of a specific instance of learning is introduced; however, it is still spoken about in terms of generalizations.

For example: You may talk about your client learning to read and begin by suggesting that children have the experience of learning to read. As you shift from children to the client's own experience, highlight milestones within the experience of learning that are general enough for you to know to be true yet feel specific in the client's memory.

Eventually, you will shift your pronouns so this early learning experience is now specifically about the client. (There is an example of this is in the next section.)

Step 3: Bringing in Detail

Now it is time to build a strong representation for the client. In this step, break the learning process down into exquisite detail. You can talk about all of the steps in learning the skill and feel free to use embedded suggestions liberally. This is typically the moment when the client will step into the regression.

Step 4: Tying It to Now

Towards the end of the set, casually link this learning experience with achieving the outcome or the next step in the process.

Example: The following transcript is an Early Learning Set used to format the unconscious mind for easily learning new things. It is the type of loop I may use with a class on the first day of training. Some of the embedded suggestions are italicized. Others are not so that your unconscious mind can enjoy them.

> The human brain is designed for learning. Every day of our lives we *learn something new*. Sometimes we consciously realize we've learned something; other times it's left with the *unconscious*. Surprisingly, when people think about learning, often they recall childhood. And they are right in knowing that childhood is a time of great exploration and learning. Most of what people know as adults comes from their experiences as children, for example, the ability to read and write. Most people who can do these things right now can do them because they learned as small children about the alphabet. For instance, when you were a small child, you learned how to read and write. I wonder if you can *recall now when you learned*. You begin by learning the letters of the alphabet and the sounds they make. You learn that an *A* has a long

sound and a short sound and a *C* can have a hard sound or a soft sound. And, of course, you practiced drawing those letters over and over again. You *pay close attention* as you practice capital and lowercase letters. There may even be some excitement there as you learn how to read the mysterious code.

You next learn to put letters together to make sounds and words; a /ca/ and /at/ make /cat/. At first, it is difficult to remember the difference between a *b* and a *d*; it's all a matter of perspective. As you *have fun* practicing your new skills, things become very easy. As you learn to read longer words, you'll forget how you learned to read the smaller words—they are just automatic. Eventually, those bigger words are just as automatic. *You're learning a skill for life.* What first takes a little conscious effort becomes easy when you *let go* and allow your mind to do what it is designed to do: learn.

Now very soon those words become stories that let you travel anywhere in your mind. You can be transported to far off planets, the bottom of the sea, or perhaps somewhere a bit closer to home where you can have adventures and *make new discoveries.* I do wonder what story you can be experiencing now that can support you and the learnings you are making.

Erickson often began this type of induction by inviting the client to fixate his gaze on some object in the distance. Then he began the loop. When using this loop for formatting the unconscious and inducing trance, it is important to remember to pace and lead your client's state through your physiology and voice. This means the further into the loop you are, the more hypnotic your tonality. In terms of hypnotic inductions, this is a tremendous contribution to the field. Erickson wasn't worried so much about the language and crafting the perfect suggestion, especially later in his career. The induction of hypnosis is the result of a symbiotic relationship. The client follows the hypnotist into trance when there is rapport and the hypnotist's nonverbal communications suggest trance.

The Early Learning Set as Therapy

If Erickson suspected that the client's issue was linked to some past event from childhood, he often did not ask the client directly about it. He assumed that if the unconscious mind believed the conscious mind was not able to handle confronting the childhood issue, then the unconscious mind communicated indirectly with the hypnotist, keeping the conscious mind out of the loop. One of the core presuppositions that Erickson held throughout his career was that "you need not make conscious what is unconscious." There is no need to force the information into conscious awareness.

Instead, Erickson would track the changes in muscle tone and breathing and when and where the client would place emphasis and pauses and alter the amount of detail being shared. He would then use this information to deduce the negative states and learnings from the past that needed to be changed to create transformation in the present.

Based on what he observed, Erickson would choose a universal childhood experience that could be used as a resource for the client now. This would create a parallel reality between the childhood resource and the learning that needed to take place either during the childhood experience being reimprinted or even instances where no childhood event was indicated by the unconscious.

For example: If the client had fear around an upcoming event, Erickson might have chosen the universal experience of children being afraid of the dark but eventually growing to cherish the peacefulness of a dark room before falling asleep at night.

This same technique was also used when Erickson did know there was a specific childhood event that needed to be reimprinted. On some occasions, he was direct and took the client back to key life events where the client could develop skills to help her through the difficult

106

moments.

For example: If there was a memory that needed to be reimprinted about something traumatic that happened at home, Erickson might take the client back to before the event but move the client into a different setting, such as a classroom or a friend's house. In that setting, Erickson suggested that his voice could become the voice of the teacher or friend or loved one. Sometimes his voice could become the gentle breeze. Erickson then proceeded to facilitate unconscious learning experiences that would help the client through the difficult memory.

Example: Following is a partial transcript of a session in which this technique was used. For clarity, this is not an excerpt from Erickson's but from my work.

This client was in his mid 20s and had developed a fear of flying at the age of 10 after the death of his grandfather. The death had no connection with flying. Before that time, he enjoyed flying. He now was required to fly internationally for his career. He is a musician who comes from a strongly spiritual family. Both are used as leverage in the change.

For brevity, I am not including the work we did before the reimprinting or the formal trance induction that was used.

> Hypnotist: There are many things you learned throughout your life to this point. When you were small, you learned important things, like how to read and write. I know you also learned music. When you are small it's easy to learn music. You first discover the sounds each key of the piano makes. You discover those keys have letters and you can put a C, an E, and a G together to make a C chord. And how magical is it to discover the secret code those letters and chords are written in on the staff sheet.

> Client: [Smiles.]

Hypnotist: There are other very important learnings that take place for a boy of 7, 8, or even 9. Wouldn't it be charming to remember some of the secret knowledge an 8- or 9-year-old has that the 25-year-old has forgotten about?

Client: [Nods.]

Hypnotist: When you are curious, it is easy to drift back in time, to become that younger you again. I don't know how you experience it, but you can certainly be aware that you are changing. For example, the world becomes big and colorful for an 8-year-old. You could be enjoying a music lesson and know that my voice will go with you. My voice can become that of your teacher's, a friend's, a loved one's, even the melody you're playing on the piano, or a comfortable breeze. I do wonder; tell me what notes are in an E chord.

Client: E, G sharp, and B.

Hypnotist: Very good. Now show me on the piano.

Client: [Slowly moves fingers.]

Hypnotist: You are learning your chords very well. [Hypnotist is taking on the role of the music teacher to help the client stabilize the regression.] What is this chord on the page?

Client: B chord.

[Hypnotist is now inviting full unconscious participation by having the client generate a part of the hallucination.]
Hypnotist: I can see you have been practicing your

music at home, and that's how the music becomes easy. You don't have to think about it; the music just flows through you into your fingers, through the keys, which creates the sound, which goes into your ears, and the circle continues—the music flowing in a loop always through you. ... Now, since you have been so diligently practicing your lessons, I have a new lesson for you, something all great musicians understand. Do you think you are ready for the secret?

Client: [Nods.]

Hypnotist: All right then. People think the beauty in music is only in the melody. They play a song focusing only on the joy that comes from the sounds. They miss out on something very important, the space between the notes. The counts between notes and chords create the beauty of the song. A song that only has a G chord is not a song at all. Listen to the space between each note. A note has a beginning, middle, and an end as determined by the musician. That note must finish in order for the new note to begin. The same is true about songs. It would be boring if you only played one song and played it continuously. Songs have beginnings, middles, and ends as well. The ending of one song means a new song can begin when the musician chooses. Of course, you know that even if the song is not being played, it still lives in the musician. Just because we can't hear the song doesn't mean it isn't still there with the musician. And it is those quiet moments between notes and songs that we can really appreciate the song. ... I know you have other things that are very important to a boy of 9 years old. [Shifts voice locus.] A boy of your age should really be learning about the world and what is beyond it. I know when I was a little girl, my grandfather had so much wisdom. I wonder what a boy of 9 can learn from his grandfather. I don't know where you are with him now, but I do know that he has something very important to teach you, a message that a boy your age could use as he goes through life. Listen closely to his words. ... [Lengthy pause to encourage the unconscious mind to take the lead in the healing process.] ... I don't know what he is telling you right now. It might be about how nothing happens in the world outside of God's design. The message could be trusting that the Divine is in control and you can trust Him to be with you. Everything is His will. ... Or it could be something that a 10-year-old boy needs because when you are 10, you are more aware of how you feel and about the natural melody of life. There may be things that you need to say to that loved one there, and there may be a message you need to receive. I don't know what those are, but you can know things are changing. ... Just as you sit at the piano and play your song, feeling the ebb and flow of the music. The song itself carrying a message from your heart, into your fingers, and received by your ears and into your heart, an ongoing conversation that brings comfort and peace.

At this point, I bring the client forward through his timeline, inviting him to notice how things are different, including the experience of flying.

The Ericksonian approach is useful with clients who do not want to go back to the events requiring reimprinting or if they are too traumatic. In the example above, I had both conscious and unconscious permission to work with the death of the grandfather but chose a more indirect route for the client's benefit. You can certainly be even more indirect with this approach as well.

The basic steps are very simple:

1. Choose a resourceful experience you know your client had as a child unrelated to the issue needing reimprinting.

2. Regress the client to a period before the event where she can associate into the positive experience.
3. Associate yourself with a key figure in that experience.
4. Use the experience as a metaphor to teach skills and understandings that will positively reimprint the problematic experience.

If you are using a number of different positive experiences to build a stacked anchor or to pace and lead the client, it is very useful to associate your voice with something like the breeze, as it gives you a nice way of transitioning from one event to the next. You may also want to change voice locus to send the clear unconscious message that the scene is changing.

Chapter 14
Reimprinting through Deep Trance Identification

Deep Trance Identification, or DTI, is a hypnotic process through which a modeler steps into the identity of a chosen model so that he may develop new unconscious skills, states, beliefs, and values. DTI is a useful tool for both therapeutic and generative change. In this chapter, I focus on how you can use it as a regression to create both types of change.

(For a more in-depth approach to this life-changing technique, please read *Deep Trance Identification: Unconscious Modeling and Mastery for Hypnosis Practitioners, Coaches, and Everyday People* by Shawn Carson, Jess Marion, with John Overdurf.)

Why DTI?

The simple answer to this is that it is wired into our brain and our DNA. Our brain is designed to learn through the experiences of others. Mirror neurons are constantly working to allow us to have similar biochemical experiences as those with whom we are in rapport. You have probably had the experience of watching a movie or reading a book and connecting with the characters deeply enough to feel their emotions. This is what makes dramas tear jerkers and horror films scary.

Small children learn primarily through DTI. They identify with the adults in their lives, fictional heroes, and archetypal forms, such as a firefighter or doctor. They then play out elaborate scenarios being those characters. From the average adult perspective, it looks like "just playing." In reality, however, children are learning basic cultural values, skills such as problem solving and counting or how to interact in an adult world.

The human brain is wired to learn quickly through Deep Trance Identification.

Across the span of history, DTI appears in countless cultures—from the trance dancers of Bali to the daemons of ancient Greece to Stanislovski's method acting. DTI has been with us for thousands of years. Learning in this way has left a genetic imprint that replicates itself with each new generation.

Deep Trance Identification is one of the most powerful tools for enacting deep and lasting generative change.

Generative Regression through DTI

In the 1960s, Vladimir Raikov, a Soviet researcher, began experimenting with DTI for skills acquisition. His papers (available in Russian) are the earliest record we have found of a codified and systematic approach to DTI.

Before we jump into the technique itself, I invite you to imagine the scene. It is the 1960s, the height of the Cold War. The Soviet Union and the United States are in not only an arms race but also a race to be the top in the sciences and arts. Raikov is enlisted by the Party to use hypnosis with young musicians at the Moscow Conservatory, one of the most prestigious music schools in the world. Raikov agrees, under the condition that it be set up as an experiment so that he could track the success of his techniques.

Raikov divided the students into three groups. The first group (the control) underwent no hypnosis. The second group experienced hypnotic relaxation techniques. The third group went through Raikov's DTI protocol using exemplary musicians and their instruments. For example, a pianist may use DTI with Rachmaninoff.

At the end of the year, students took a performance exam in their instrument. They were graded both on technique and artistic interpretation. Students who went through relaxation techniques scored higher than the control group. Interestingly, the DTI group scored significantly better than the other two groups in both categories.

Throughout this book, you have seen references to both therapeutic and generative change. *Therapeutic change* refers to issues clients come in with that they want "fixed," such as anxiety, smoking cessation, nail biting. *Generative change work* is more focused on long-term transformation for the client. This is about moving towards a goal as opposed to away from a problem.

Traditionally, DTI has been used primarily as a generative process focused almost exclusively on skills acquisition. The technique provided below can certainly be used as a therapeutic process or as method of skills acquisition. I encourage you to also think about it as a meta-skill the client can use to aid in her journey of personal evolution well beyond discrete skills development.

While both techniques presented in this chapter can be used as standalone process, they are most effective as a part of long-term DTI modeling project.

The Generative Technique

Begin by having the client choose the specific context in which the skill will be used. This grounds the experience and creates environmental anchors for the skill and state once in the outside world.

Next, help the client to find a model that represents the skills he would like to acquire or reflects who that person wants to become. The model can be real or fictional. The result depends more on the level of rapport the client has with the model than with the realistic nature of the model or the model's biography. This selection can be done consciously or unconsciously.

It's important that you and your client have a familiarity with the model's biography and your client is specific in the context and desired outcome. Be very clear as to the desired outcome, and check both its ecology and its achievability. If a client wants to come out of this experience playing like Jimmy Hendrix but has never picked up a guitar in his life, the odds are he will be disappointed at the end. If, however, you have a guitarist looking to expand his ability or explore a new style comfortably, the outcome makes more sense.

For ecology reasons, before moving forward, check in with the client's unconscious mind that this model is agreeable. To further ensure ecology, you may also choose to have the client's unconscious mind choose the model. (Details on how to do both are available in our *Deep Trance Identification* book.)

Once the context, outcome, and model are chosen, move on to the regression.

Step 1: Regress the Client

This step is fairly straightforward at this point. You can use any of the methods presented in this book as well as direct approaches. Direct approaches might be to count the client back through the years, to look backward through the book or photo album of her life, or to use simple suggestion. The method is less important as long as the client can experience a revivification or regression.

To what point you should regress your client depends on your judgment and the client's needs. In the original Raikov regression, musicians went back to early childhood. When I use this pattern, I typically invite the client's unconscious mind to find a pleasant memory from early childhood around the age of 4 or 5. This gives the opportunity for years of iteration of the skills while in trance. It also loosens the conscious grip on the process. It is difficult for most people to pinpoint the specific age within a memory of being 4 or 5 unless it is something holding a lot of emotional energy. More than likely the client will step into some pleasant experience that the unconscious approximates to be in that age range. When the memory appears, most clients fully engage with it instead of being overly critical, hence the regression.

Step 2: Association

The easiest mechanism for transitioning into the model is the use of *perceptual positions.* Perceptual positions are the idea that as a consciousness, you can move into different perspectives. There are traditionally three positions we can inhabit; (H)NLP has introduced a fourth.

The first position is you as yourself seeing through your own eyes. Second position is being in someone else's shoes. You could imagine stepping into your friend's shoes and seeing through his eyes, hearing through his ears, and looking back at you. Third position is more dissociated. You can think of this like being a butterfly in the corner of the room. You can see your physical form, other people's bodies, and everything else happening around you. Fourth position is sometimes described as the system in which we are a part. It is also the space between you and everyone else. Imagine sitting in a comfortable place with a good friend. You can become aware of the physical space that surrounds the two of you as well as the space between you both. As a consciousness, you can step into that space between you and your friend and become aware of the flow of energy between you both.

To help the client associate into her model, first guide her in stepping outside of herself as a consciousness. You will be moving the person into third position—she can see herself and the model. Later this will be very important as a final ecology step.

From third position, the modeler can associate fully into the model. Use the same tools of association that you used in other regression techniques to help the client fully step into being a model. You want to ground her in the physiological experience of being in the model's form as well as the environment around them. Suggest that the client look back at the person she's sharing the space with. From here on, refer to the client by the model's name. And anytime the model interacts with the form of the client, use the client's name and not the pronoun *you*. This is similar to the dissociation step during the traditional conversational regression.

Here is where things get interesting. The question arises as to whether you associate the client into the child form or the adult form of her model. The limited translations of Raikov's papers are ambiguous around this detail. Feel free to experiment with both. You may find that the approach you choose will depend on the clients and their specific goals.

Step 3: Growing Skills

Just as in the previous steps, you have some options as to how to proceed. The first two are used when having the modeler associate into the child version of the model. Option 1 is to help the client grow up through the client's own timeline as the model. This means that the musician who identifies with Rachmaninoff will go through all of the experiences the musician had in childhood and adolescence but doing so as Rachmaninoff. Option 2 is that the client steps into the child version of the model and grows up through the model's timeline. This means that the musician becomes Rachmaninoff and grows up through the experiences that Rachmaninoff had.

Alternatively, you can have the client, as a child, associate into the adult model. In this approach, the model stays with the representation of the client and watches the client grow up through the years offering advice to the client when needed and teaching the desired skills. This version creates a split awareness between being the client growing up through the years and the model who is doing the coaching.

Any of these variations can be highly generative. I have used all three with different clients with highly generative outcomes.

Step 4: Motion

Raikov added a step that forever changed how I do Deep Trance Identification. As the modeler was growing and practicing the skills, Raikov would elicit unconscious movement in the hands. A musician would play a hallucinated version of her or his instrument. The fingers and hands would become active at this part of the hypnotic session.

The reason this is so pivotal is that it introduces the motor cortex into the learning process. The motor cortex is the crossroads of the brain. When activating the motor cortex, it becomes very easy to activate multiple other centers of the brain simultaneously. This is a quick way of creating a tremendous amount of neurological leverage.

We utilize a similar technique during the DTI regression process. If the client is using the DTI regression for discrete skills acquisition, you can have him practice the skill while deeply associated into the model. If the client is interested in a transformation that cannot be acted out physically—such as a change in beliefs, values, and identity—you can utilize other forms of movement. The easiest and most common unconscious movement is arm levitation. As the client experiences the model growing through the years, you can induce arm levitation and use that as an external gauge for where the client is in the process as well as activating the motor cortex, which will automatically make the client more resourceful.

Step 5: Dissociation

Once the modeler has reached his current age as the model, you can either dissociate the modeler now or, if the model's timeline extends later in life, you can have the modeler go through those experiences that happened after the current age.

For example: If you were modeling Milton Erickson as a 30-year-old, you may want to experience being Erickson when he was in his 60s or

70s. Whichever approach you choose is fine as long as you remember to bring the modeler back to the modeler's current age before dissociating.

When you're ready to dissociate, have the modeler step outside of the model into third position. Give the suggestion that the modeler will take all of the useful learning from this experience, and that anything that is not resourceful that belongs to the model can stay with the model. Remember, I mentioned that third position would be important again for ecology reasons. You use this position as a place of rest before transitioning into the next phase.

Step 6: Fourth Position

This step does not belong to the original Raikov pattern and is an addition from John Overdurf. Invite the modeler, as a consciousness, to become aware of the space between the model and the modeler and to allow their awareness to fill that space to feel the connection between the two of them. This is a nice way of deepening rapport between model and modeler, especially if the modeler is interested in doing more DTI experiences with the model. It also indirectly reconfirms that ultimately the model and the modeler are connected and the model is, in reality, a part of the modeler.

Step 7: Reassociation

The last step of this process is to have the client fully associate back into his body. A nice way of closing this experience is by inviting the client to thank the model for sharing this journey with him. Then bring the client out of trance, offering any positive suggestions you feel will benefit him.

Therapeutic DTI Regression

The first type of therapeutic regression I present here does not require extensive knowledge of the model's biography as long as the client has a strong emotional connection with the model. The model will be the one to reimprint the client's memory. Use this version of the DTI regression on a specific event in the client's past.

This approach is ideal for clients who have difficulty seeing themselves as being resourceful, are afraid to address the past, or who enjoy fantasy worlds.

The technique is very simple. Have the client choose a model that the younger version of herself looked up to. If the client cannot think of one, or if the model no longer has a strong emotional connection for the client, she can choose a current model she does have a connection to. It is key here that the model create a strongly positive state to the client. The model must be bigger than the problem or event.

Step 1: Meeting the Model

After the induction, ask the modeler to meet the model in a comfortable space for the modeler. This can be an inner sanctuary, someplace special to the client, or somewhere connected with comfort. After greeting the model, the client shows the model the problematic memory. This might be done in a crystal ball, iPad screen, smartphone, or any other small device. The representation of the memory should be small in this part in the process. Remember that the submodality of size will impact the emotional response to the events being shown.

Step 2: Association

Just as with the previous DTI experience, use the perceptual positions to navigate the client into the experience of the model. Move the client from first position into third position and finally into second position as the model. It is crucial, at this stage, that you associate the client fully into the experience of the model. This is not just seeing through the model's eyes but also experiencing the model's beliefs, thoughts, emotions, values, and identity. Suggest the modeler fully experience everything that makes that model resourceful.

Step 3: Reimprinting

The model now goes back in time to visit the event that needs to be reimprinted. The visual representation of the modeler's body can remain in the comfortable space. Once the model finds the event, it is the model's job to coach the younger self through the experience. Just as with the standard reimprinting, it is essential that the model fully access the positive states first and then gift them to the younger self.

The model begins by resourcing the younger self before moving on to the other participants in the memory.

The model watches the memory play through after each instance of resourcing, making any changes and adding any new resources that will make the difference in that moment for the client.

Step 4: Returning

After the memory is resourced, the model returns to the space where the client at her current age is and notices how that client is different. Ask the model to describe the change that she sees in the client. This is a not-so-indirect suggestion to the client that she has, in fact, changed. The model now shows the client the new memory on the same screen. If any other changes need to occur, anything the model missed in the event, the client can point it out and the model goes back to the event and adds in those resources.

Step 5: Integration

Once the memory has changed to the point where the client is now comfortable and has changed, if it is appropriate, the client can go back in time and experience the new memory. This is done by first inviting the client's consciousness to dissociate from the model, being sure to move through third position.

Going forward, keep in mind that new memory includes the coaching and resourcing from the model. You're introducing a new element into the old memory. I recognize that some people might be concerned about creating a false memory. With this type of technique, the client's unconscious mind knows the perceived real event from the hypnotic event. Often the unconscious mind creates a difference in visual submodalities between the events that took place in the outside world and the event taking place in the client's mind in that moment.

As a part of the integration, the coach asks the client to step into first position in the memory and experience the coaching from that position. This is done for two reasons. The first is that it gives the client the opportunity to integrate the new emotional experience of the memory while being coached through it. This creates an added resourceful part that the client could call upon in other contexts if he chooses. The second reason is that it gives the client the opportunity for iteration of the reimprinting. What ends up being reprinted in the second go-through from the first position will be slightly different from the experience as the model. You are stacking resources onto that memory.

When the time is right, you see that the client's physiology is symmetrical and a positive state is held as he goes through the event. Grow him up through the years with this newfound resourcefulness. Grow him to the point of being an adult in the comfortable space with the model.

The final part of the integration is to invite the model to integrate fully into the client. The metaphor here is that the client has all of the resources available to the model. This also ensures a full integration among the client, the memory, and the resources.

There may be some instances where it is not appropriate for the client, even as the model, to go back to the event. In these cases, you can still use the pattern with some modification. Associate the client into the model to watch the event play out on the tiny screen, being sure to build up a strong link with the model's resources. Then dissociate the client from the model and associate him back into himself watching the little screen in the comfortable place. The model then can go back and reimprint the younger version of the client while the client observes from a place of comfort.

This variation is far more Ericksonian in that you place full trust in the client's unconscious mind that it knows how to make the change. Your client may need some preframes established before this pattern about the power of his unconscious mind and how easily and quickly it can make lasting changes.

Covert Reimprinting through Superheroes

You can also use DTI as a method of indirect reimprinting. There are occasions when clients are not interested in going back to past events that are contributing to current issues. In these instances, I typically use a DTI with either a superhero or a supervillain. While this may not be appropriate for every client, superheroes play an important role in popular imagining and culture. And most people have a favorite superhero in one form or another. The benefit of choosing this type of fictional character is that most children grow up with a favorite superhero. So when you invite a client to meet that superhero and associate in, you are inviting the client to regress to childhood. The real networks associated with that superhero are also linked with the client's childhood. When you do this, you will see a shift in the client's physiology into a resourceful and regressed state when he meets the model then into a highly resourceful state as the model. This type of reimprinting is done completely via metaphor. To construct this metaphor, I typically use symbolic modeling questions.

(If you're not familiar with this process, it was developed by Penny Tompkins and James Lawley. There are number of resources available online. And you can find an example of this as applied to Deep Trance Identification in the DTI book.)

Supervillains also are useful models for DTI and regression. Just as with superheroes, they initialize an automatic unconscious regression. One of the key areas that supervillains have a leg up on superheroes is in the world of team building. Supervillains seem to always make friends with other supervillains. This gives them access to far more resources than one person normally has. You can use this strategy as a regression as well as a six-step reframe. The supervillain also becomes a proxy for the problem state and behavior. Clients often look at problems as being the "bad guy" in the story of the client's life. Utilizing supervillains reframes that to something useful.

Outside of using symbolic modeling questions, the process for this type of regression is simple. After discussing the specific change the client would like to experience, and any relevant memories associated with the problem, dissociate the client through the hypnotic induction. From here, you can associate the client into the superhero or supervillain through the perceptual positions.

At this point, you have a lots of freedom to play. You can invite the client to create scenarios, landscapes, and adventures to be on as the superhero. Ideally, you cocreate this hypnotic environment with the client. As the client experiences the adventures, you can use embedded suggestions and Milton Model language to help the unconscious mind apply the learnings being made within the superhero environment to the change and any relevant memories in the client's life. Because you have activated the problem state and any relevant memories before this experience, in most instances, the unconscious mind will automatically already be drawing conclusions and making connections. This is particularly true if you do not tell the client what you're doing. As far as the client's conscious mind is concerned, he is having a very unusual hypnotic adventure. Remember that dopamine is released through novel experiences, so you're already creating a strong resource for your client. Meanwhile, his unconscious mind is looking for the meaning in the experience. It will be making meaning out of it and applying it where needed.

This chapter is just a taste of what you can do with Deep Trance Identification in respect to regression work or any other type of transformation. We began by discussing the differences between therapeutic and generative change. When you use DTI, the line between therapeutic change and generative change disappears. All therapeutic change ultimately becomes generative change because your clients are learning a lot more from the model than they can consciously realize at any given moment. DTI becomes a tool for life that can help with any type of new learning that the client is interested in.

So I invite you to let go of the distinction between therapeutic and generative even though we have made a distinction for ease of understanding within this book. For your clients, all change is generative because even the smallest therapeutic change can have a lifetime of positive far-reaching effects.

Chapter 15
Reimprinting for Smokers:
The Smoking Destroyer

Smoking cessation is the cornerstone of many successful hypnosis and coaching practices. It is vitally important that change-workers have the ability to work successfully with smokers. Fortunately, smoking cessation can be one of the easiest yet most fulfilling types of change work a hypnotist does.

If you already have a smoking cessation program, feel free to integrate this technique to the extent it makes sense for you. If you are new to smoking cessation, this pattern is one piece of a larger process. This is not the only thing I do with smokers nor is it the first.

Understanding the Smoking Habit

Despite what we have been led to believe by the pharmaceutical industry, quitting does not need to be difficult nor a lengthy process filled with pills, patches, gums, and e-cigarettes. While nicotine, a harsh stimulant, does contribute to the habit, ultimately, it is the interaction of a number of intrapersonal factors that creates the habit.

For our purposes, we will focus on one of those factors, the type of problem the client has. Generally speaking, clients have one of two types of problems:

1. Cause and effect
2. Complex equivalence

Cause-and-effect problems are constructed when the client attributes the problem to a specific trigger. *For example*: A client might say, "I get nervous every time I have to speak in public." Speaking in public is the cause and feeling nervous is the effect.

A complex equivalence is slightly different. This is what Korzybski referred to as a confusion of levels of abstraction (logical levels). The client takes the problematic state or behavior and applies it to her identity. These types of problems are often stated as an "I am" statement.

For example: A client might say, "I am anxious." *Anxious* is not an identity, yet the client has constructed as such through the words she has chosen.

Smokers hold their problem into place by creating both cause–effect relationships and complex equivalences. When the smoker comes into the office, she has a number of reasons why she smokes. Most of the reasons are linked to daily stress and the perceived relaxation that comes from the habit. Many of these reasons can be reframed quite easily. There is, however, one cause–effect that often goes unnoticed. This is the original cause–effect that led the smoker to smoking in the first place. This cause–effect relationship might be that she watched her parents smoking during childhood, her friends smoked, or she wanted to fit in with the group. Somewhere in the neural networks associated with the habit is a memory still looping about that original cigarette experience that is helping hold the problem in place.

Along with this, the client has spent many years crafting an identity for herself in relationship to the cigarette. These clients will say, "I am a smoker." This statement has, in one short breath, taken a habit and moved it up to the sum total of that person's identity. Smoking is an activity, not an identity.

(As an aside: In this book and elsewhere, you will note that I use the identity level word *smoker* for brevity and to keep readers on the same page. In sessions, however, identity-level statements are used only when that identity is resourceful.)

When to Use This Pattern in a Smoking-Cessation Session

The Smoking Destroyer Pattern is powerful form of reimprinting that diminishes the original cause of the client's habit and then alters her identity, thus changing the complex equivalences the client is making in relation to her self.

You will help the client to make a fundamental identity change, which means that there are certain places in a session where this pattern makes more sense to be done. I typically consider this the tipping point. Once the client successfully goes through this process, she is fully a nonsmoker. Everything else we do after is cleanup of the mindless behavior of smoking. This pattern is ideally placed later in your session. It will not make much sense to run this pattern before any aversion work or fork-in-the-road patterns.

The Process

Step 1: Changing the Movie

Before beginning this pattern, it is important to find out whether the client enjoyed her first cigarette.

Begin by having the client imagine being in a comfortable movie theater. Take some time to fully build up the sensory experience of this space. Once in the space, the client can find that the large movie screen in front of her begins to play the memory of the first cigarette. This movie should be dissociated—meaning the client can see her younger self interacting in that event. If you know the client did not enjoy her first cigarette, invite the client to step into the movie and experience that memory again from the inside out. As she is doing this, feel free to place a cigarette in her hand. You create a negative anchor between the experience and the cigarette. Take your time to build up this negative experience.

If, on the other hand, the client enjoyed her first cigarette, do not have her associate in. Instead, she will watch the movie from the movie theater. It is far more rare for a client to have enjoyed the first cigarette. If the client cannot remember whether she liked it, keep her dissociated. You do not want to associate a client into enjoying a cigarette.

Once the movie has ended, if the client was associated into the experience, bring her back into the movie theater. The movie will begin again, but this time help the client to make submodality shifts. Guide her to drain the color from the movie, making it black and white. The client can speed the movie up and run it forwards and backwards while distorting the image. Fade any light from the movie so that it becomes grainy and dark. Finally, shrink the movie down so it is barely perceptible, and move it into the distance and into the client's past.

The implication here is that you and the client are getting rid of that old useless movie and creating something new on that screen.

Step 2: Resourcing

Next, the client will invite a much younger version of herself into the theater. I typically use some time within the imprinting phase of the client's life, generally around 7 years old. Clients tend to begin smoking in their teenage years. But it is very difficult to resource teenagers, as they often do not want to listen to adults. It is much easier to resource a 7-year-old whose filters are still open. This also means, metaphorically, that between the ages of 7 and whenever that first cigarette is offered, they will have had many years of practicing the new resources.

When the younger self comes into the theater, establish a connection between the adult and younger version of the client on an emotional level. The adult client then proceeds to resource for the younger self. She can do this in a similar manner to a standard reimprinting, or the adult can actively teach the child new skills and how to say no.

Earlier in my stop-smoking sessions, I teach clients Emotional Freedom Techniques to help them manage cravings. At this point in the pattern, I encourage the adult to teach the child the same strategy. You can do this with any self-hypnosis technique you teach the client before this pattern. This not only gives the adult a solid skill to teach the younger version but also reinforces the technique that you previously taught the client. You're helping him to commit the technique to memory.

The client can offer any useful advice or encouragement. What is important here is that the adult client accesses positive states and, on another level, commits to the change.

Step 3: The New Movie

After the child is fully resourced, it is time to watch a new movie. Both the client and her younger self can sit in the theater and watch the movie of the first time she was offered a cigarette. This will be the same memory as the one that you worked with at the beginning of this pattern. This time, however, the client will say no. During the resourcing phase, the client will have taught the younger self how to say no. The new movie is the opportunity to watch that play out on the big screen.

As the client watches this movie—where she, in fact, says no and remains a nonsmoker—you, as the hypnotist, will take time to build up her self-esteem. Typically, I ask the client, "How does it feels to watch that teenage self in that movie say no and make a better choice?" The typical response is that the client feels proud. Really build up the positive state. Allow the movie to continue past the point of the initial incident so that the client can watch all the key moments of her life until now and see how she has been transformed because she is a nonsmoker. That means each time in her life when a cigarette was offered in the past, she can now say no.

When you see the client is in a big positive state, feel free to ask her if she would like to watch that movie again and feel even better. You can run this movie loop as many times as you want, and each time the client can enjoy watching herself be strong, independent, and living the type of life she wants.

I usually run this movie two or three times, depending on how big a state the client is experiencing. If the client is in a massively positive state, and really getting into watching the movie, we may play it three or more times. If the client isn't in a really great state, but there's a sense to keep things moving, then twice will generally do at this point.

At this point, as long as you did a good job in the movie-screen process, the client will not fail to access a positive state. If, for some reason, she does not, you will need to take a step back and become curious as to whether the client really wants to quit or if there is something blocking her from seeing herself as a nonsmoker.

Step 4: Integration

Finally, it is time to integrate the adult, the child, and the teenager in the movie. Do this one step at a time. First, the child is integrated. Before saying good-bye to the younger self, the client is encouraged to share any words of wisdom or anything else that the child needs that will make a difference growing up as a nonsmoker.

Next, the child walks up to the movie screen and steps into it and become the teenager. So the 7-year-old will merge with the 14- or 15-year-old. The client then watches the movie one more time enjoying all the positive states associated with it.

Finally, the client steps inside the movie and associates into the younger self of 14 or 15 years of age and experiences what it's like to say no to all the cigarettes that would've otherwise been in her life.

Grow the client up through the years really enjoying saying no to every cigarette offered.

This is a powerful pattern for helping someone create a new identity. The most frequent comment clients make after experiencing this pattern is that while they can remember being a smoker, it feels like it's not a *part* of them. They often report feeling as though the smoking was something foreign and, on some occasions, even report that they were never a smoker in the first place.

In the very rare occasion that a client reports not remembering smoking, it is important for you, as the hypnotist, to address the issue of the system that the client exists in. Regardless of what the client may or may not remember about the habit, the people in his life will remember him as a smoker. Family members and friends may try to bring back the old habit by casting doubt on the change the client has experienced or making comments about the old identity the client believed he had. You can easily address these issues hypnotically as well as in the conversations you have with the client. It is important to create a separation between who the client is and who those close to him remember him as being before the session.

Chapter 16
Reimprinting Others

Up to this point, we have explored the power of reimprinting a client's past to create a happier life now and into the future. It is fairly obvious that once a client changes, her relationships change and she will indirectly help others change.

For example: A person who reimprints a traumatic event from her past will find great freedom and happiness today, and that will influence her interactions with her children and, subsequently, how those children experience the world.

What would happen for a client, though, if you were to help reimprint an event from someone else's life? How would a client be personally impacted if his parent or grandparent had some trauma reimprinted? The client would be different because the interactions within the family system would have changed.

While it may not be possible to go back in time and change events of someone in the client's life, it is possible to change the internal representations that client has of that other person, thus changing the system and helping the client in his personal evolution.

Case Study

Several years ago I had a client I will call "Jane." Jane wanted more confidence and a higher sense of self-esteem. She shared that when she was young, her mother had attempted to murder her father. The issue was not the trauma of that event but the long-term ramifications of it, primarily the incarceration of the mother in a psychiatric facility, which had led Jane to develop a deep sense of guilt. She felt guilty because she was not able to have the type of relationship with the mother that she thought the two should have had. She also felt a deep sense of guilt because the mother was the victim of sexual abuse as a child and the subsequent violent behavior Jane believed to be a result of that abuse. She wished someone could have been there to help her mother so maybe things would be different now.

When asked how she wanted to be different in respect to her mother, Jane wanted to be free of the guilt surrounding her mother's past as well as the guilt linked to not being able, up to that point, to have a relationship with the mother.

The pattern I present below was the cornerstone of the work we did together. While it was not the only technique used through our sessions together, this was the turning point for Jane.

The Technique

This technique is ideal for clients who have created cause–effect relationships between events that have happened to other people and the client's current issue, or for the client who has given events that happened to another person unresourceful meanings (complex equivalences) that impact the client.

Step 1: Preframes

While many of the preframes given before this pattern are the same as the preframes you would use typically before every reimprinting, I spend a few moments here to address some additional useful preframes. These additional preframes may help with the client's full conscious and unconscious participation in the process. Because you will be reimprinting someone else, not the client, there is the risk that the client's conscious mind will object. Adding these preframes will help sidestep this.

The first preframe is around the idea that you're not changing the actual events that happened to the client's loved one or the events that occurred between the client and that person. Instead, you are helping the client to change how she *feels* about that other person and how she interprets interactions with that person. This is about changing the client's internal representations of a loved one and her interactions, thus creating greater freedom in the client's life.

Connected with this is the preframe of this experience being solely about the client. You're using this pattern because this will help the client to achieve her therapeutic goals. This is not about trying to change the loved one in the outside world. We have to be very clear with the client at this point that while she will, in fact, change her own experience of her loved one, it is not her job to try to change the loved one in the outside world. This is primarily for reasons of ecology. It may not be ecological for the client to run around trying to change others. Alternatively, the client gets to enjoy how the relationship may change organically.

The final preframe is about resourcefulness. Take some time to demonstrate to the client how resourceful she actually is and how she can use that resourcefulness to help others. This pattern places the client in the position of responsibility for helping others. As you set up this preframe, calibrate the client's unconscious response. If there is any hesitation at the idea of helping the loved one, this is a red flag that needs to be investigated further. If there are objections to any of these additional preframes, slow down and take time to investigate. It may be that a simple reframe is an order, or it could be that this pattern is not appropriate at that particular time and the client has some other work to do first.

Step 2: Psuedo-orientation in Time and Space

When you're ready to move forward, induce trance in any way you choose. Once the client is in trance, create a pseudo-orientation in time and space. This means to dissociate the client from her physical form in the present moment so that, as a consciousness, she is free to travel outside of her own timeline. In other versions of reimprinting, we use the client's states as the catalyst for the regression. Because you're going to reimprint someone else, the client can stay as an adult; however, a mechanism for transitioning through time is required.

An easy way to do this is to invite the client to step out of herself as an awareness so that she can see her body in the room with you and can see you and the rest of the room. At this point, you may want to introduce some Ericksonian-style language to help the client further dissociate. You can guide the client to finding herself in some space outside of the normal boundaries of time and space. Or you can keep it more open ended, as Erickson did, and have the client meet you in the middle of "know where."

From this place, the client is free to move backwards through time on anyone's timeline. The client can travel backwards in time on that specific loved one's timeline to sometime before the key event.

Step 3: Creating a Sanctuary

Encourage the client to create a sanctuary where she can meet with the loved one. The client will create a space in which she can introduce herself to that loved one before the event to be reprinted. In the case I presented above, the sanctuary was a classroom with lots of toys because the client was reimprinting a little girl around the age of 8 or 9.

In this space, the client can introduce herself and begin to build a bond with the other person. At this point, it is useful to create an emotional connection between both the client and the loved one.
The important point here is to make the space comfortable, safe, and appropriate for both the client and the loved one being reprinted.

Step 4: Coaching and Resourcing

Now it is time for the reimprinting. You have a number of options of how to do this. The client may choose to utilize the sanctuary as the main place for the reimprinting or join the loved one in the event guiding the loved one through it. This will depend mainly on the type of situation being reimprinted. In the case of Jane, it was completely inappropriate for her to watch the child form of her mother go through abuse. Instead, the sanctuary space became the space where the work could be done. In other situations, it may be appropriate for the client to see the event to help with the reprinting.

The reimprinting may be done in a similar way to the traditional reimprinting, where the client sends resource states to the loved one, or it may be completed through coaching. In Jane's case, she coached her mother over a number of instances between the moments of abuse. She was there for her mother in the moments immediately before the abuse and then the moments after. In those times, she would speak with the child offering her friendship, love, and support. Remember, the goal here isn't to erase the event from history; instead, it is to help the client relate to the love one and a more resourceful matter.

In cases where it is appropriate for the client to join the loved one in the situation, the client can coach the loved one through the event, or send resource states into the loved one, and the event that would make the difference for the client in the present moment.

Step 5: Temporal Integration

If the client has joined the love one in the event, the client can watch the event play through again and notice how it is different for the loved one and for the client. If it is not appropriate for the client to be present, there is no need to run the event more than once.

At this point, it will be useful to reintegrate the client into her own timeline, particularly in respect to the loved one. If the event happened before the client was born, you can certainly grow the loved one through the years until the point of meeting the client for the first time. The client can associate into herself growing through the years knowing this individual and having many different experiences together and noticing how things are different. Grow the client up to her current age in the office with you.

Although the point of this pattern is not to change external events, the client's perspective will change. During the temporal integration, the client will begin to pay more attention to the positive moments shared with that loved one.

One of the wonderful side effects of this pattern is that it tends to create forgiveness without the need for preframing forgiveness or the final piece of the reimprinting process. When clients come out of this experience, they often have a newfound respect and love not just for the loved one but also for themselves.

After Jane had gone through this experience, she reported a week later that for the first time in her adult life, she felt truly free to be herself. She no longer felt burdened by the events of her childhood or the events that had happened to her mother. It was as if Jane was reborn. She looked happier and sounded very different.

Chapter 17
Experimental Reimprinting Utilizing Implicit Memory Formation

Up to this point, we have explored the reimprinting of episodic memory through the elicitation of resource states. These resource states already have powerful neural networks linked to them that contain other episodic memories. We stack states and memories to essentially overwhelm the negative charge of the problematic memory.

The traditional approaches to regression work, as it exists in other forms, and in reimprinting, as presented here, focus solely on episodic memory. Unlike episodic memory, which is consolidated in the hippocampus alone, researchers believe implicit memory, and particularly procedural memory, may be formed and consolidated in other parts of the brain, including the motor cortex.

Procedural memory gives us the opportunity to leverage aspects of our clients' experiences and behaviors that are resourceful, automatic, and most often outside of the clients' awareness.

This chapter presents three strategies for reimprinting implicit memories. Two techniques were developed by John Overdurf. The other is an adaptation from the work of Dr. Jeffery Schwartz.

Technique 1: Reimprinting Episodic Memory through Implicit Memory Creation

I first came across this method of reimprinting in John Overdurf's "Reconsolidating Memories" audio recording (https://stores.modularmarket.com/johnoverdurf/reconsolidating-memories-p132.php). This approach uses the creation of a new procedural memory to override the physiological response from a problematic episodic memory. You will be leveraging the procedural memory's ability to create a strong physiological response that is counter to the one created by the episodic memory. This approach relies solely on physiology as opposed to asking the client what would have made the difference for him.

Creating and Installing a New Procedural Memory

Since procedural memories are embodied and typically unconscious, to create a new one, give the client a simple physical task that can easily be transitioned from conscious doing to unconscious being. You may be curious as to what I mean by *doing* versus *being*. The primary difference here is that doing requires conscious effort and, in the case of encoding procedural memories, repetition. Once the new memory has been consolidated, the conscious mind no longer needs to think about doing. Instead, the new behavior will be automatically triggered by something in the external environment. In NLP terms, this is an anchor. When this occurs, the client is just being. No conscious effort or episodic thought is triggered.

One of the easiest procedures to install is breath rhythm. Breathing is unconscious throughout most of our lives, which means learning and encoding a new rhythm will be far quicker than learning a whole new behavior.

Studies have shown that different breathing rhythms have various effects on neural activity. Certain rhythms can induce elevated heart rates and stress. Other rhythms create greater relaxation and increase the occurrences of alpha, theta, delta, and gamma brainwaves (all associated with rest and well-being). Creating a procedural memory that automatically induces a physiological state of well-being will have a tremendous healing effect on unresourceful episodic memories.

The breathing strategy that we will be installing comes from HeartMath. Their practice is to inhale and exhale for five heart beats each. Students are taught to tune in to their heart rhythm, or to at least approximate it, by counting to five evenly for each inhale and exhale. This creates a state grounded in the body and in the present moment.

While this technique is a powerful meditative tool, you want to help the client move this technique out of conscious *doing* quickly and into unconscious *being*. The quickest path to do this is through guiding and anchoring the process. Instead of inviting the client to count the breathing, the hypnotist or coach provides an external stimulus that will signal to the client when to inhale and exhale. This could be a simple raising and lowering of a hand or utilizing auditory cues. The key here is that the stimulus is consistent and easily recognizable. Using an external cue will pull the client into the present moment and later make it easier for her to access this resourceful physiology.

The installation of the memory occurs through anchoring and repetition. Give the client a few minutes to practice the resourceful physiological behavior in conjunction with the external stimulus. Next, break the state/behavior for a moment. You can easily do this by changing conversations and backing off the auditory or visual anchor, for example, stopping the lowering and raising of the hand. Calibrate the client to ensure that he is following you, meaning his physiology returns to either a more neutral state or shifts in the direction of the content of whatever you are discussing.

Now it's time to condition the response. Invite the client to engage in the resourceful behavior, and once again provide the external stimulus in conjunction with the behavior. After a few moments, back off of the anchor. This means you diminish the external stimulus while calibrating as to whether the client maintains the behavior.

Now you want to test the anchor. In the middle of a neutral conversation, fire off the anchor and calibrate as to whether the client automatically engages in the resourceful behavior. Once the anchor is set, the procedural memory is in place and you can move forward with the reimprinting.

Reimprinting the Memory

For this step, you want the client to somewhat associate into the memory. The client does not need to relive the event intensively. You simply need to bring the memory back into the hippocampus for reconsolidation to take place.

Once the negative state associated with the memory is active enough for you to see a physiological shift, you can introduce the resource. Once you see the state, fire off the anchor for the resourceful behavior. One of the benefits of using breathing is that it can naturally activate the parasympathetic nervous system, the relaxation response. As long as you have conditioned the response and created a large enough shift in physiology when setting the positive anchor, you will be able to reimprint the memory successfully by introducing this behavior into the content of the event.

Think of this as a collapsing-anchors technique. You may see, or the client may report, a moment of confusion. Confusion, in this instance, is a very powerful resource and acts as a steppingstone from the negative emotions the client had been experiencing into the resource state. This, for some people, will be a chaining-anchors experience. From there, you will notice a shift in the client's physiology into one of resourcefulness. After a few iterations, the confusion will diminish and the resource physiology and state will be present.

Keeping in mind that repetition is your friend, run this pattern two or three more times with the anchor. Each time you run it introduce the anchor earlier in the process. You will quickly get to the point where the memory triggers the resourceful behavior and, consequently, state. This doesn't mean that the client has to feel really good about the fact that she made it through and grew as a result of the event. What it does mean is that the emotional charge diminishes from the memory.

While in the primary approach to reimprinting, invite the client to resource the participants in the event, thus reframing the client's own experience as well as the experience of others. In this version, we can offer reframes for both the client and others both there and not there in the memory. Between each iteration of the collapsing anchor, introduce useful reframes around the client's experience as well as the actions of others. This serves as a strong enough break state to ensure that the collapse doesn't run the other way. It gives you, as the hypnotist, the opportunity to indirectly suggest and build up the client's inner resourcefulness.

Once you're certain the memory has been reimprinted, the memory will trigger resourceful behaviors and states and you can move on to the final part of this process. Up to this point, the client has made—either consciously or unconsciously—the remembered event something that stands out in his own biography. Up to this point, for the client, it was a significant event that had lasting implications. On a neurological level, the client has created a border around this memory by connecting it to networks that deemed this event significant. You don't necessarily want to take away the significance of the event; however, it may be more useful for the meaning of the event to be reframed.

The easiest path to doing this is to ask the client's unconscious mind to take any and all important lessons learned from this event so that the event can be let go of. Typically, when a client has a reoccurring issue, some important message is hidden within it. Now is the time to invite that message to come forward. It's not important whether the client consciously knows what that message is. It is important, however, that you calibrate the client's physiology so that you know the meaning made at the unconscious level is resourceful. You will know this because the physiology will reflect a positive state.

Amnesia

Finally, you want the memory to resemble other memories from the client's past that contain little emotional charge. For most people, memories that no longer have emotion attached to them are very frequently not recalled. If asked about the event, a person could bring it back to conscious awareness. But it is not something that the client frequently calls to mind and, in fact, often forgets to remember. You can create a similar effect by suggesting amnesia.

Keep in mind that as you do this form of reimprinting, and any version of State-Based Coaching, your client will enter into various levels of trance automatically. You can do reimprinting after a formal hypnotic induction, but it's not necessary. As you calibrate your client, you will become aware of the instances where she dropped spontaneously into trance. You can also indirectly elicit trance states through embedded suggestions and other techniques. By the end of the reimprinting, your client will be in a pleasant trance state, which means you can take the opportunity to provide lots of positive suggestions. Some of those being around the idea of amnesia. If you are new to the practice of hypnotic amnesia, here are a couple of pointers to keep in mind.

Confusion

Confusion is an easy way of eliciting spontaneous amnesia. The classic clichéd confusion suggestions for amnesia are "You can forget to remember" or "You can remember to forget." There are a number of linguistic tools you can use to create amnesia, such as ambiguities, Markov chains, and Attention Shifting Coaching skills.

Keep in mind that there are two types of confusion, unconscious confusion and conscious confusion. Unconscious confusion occurs when neither the conscious nor unconscious mind can make sense of what's being asked. This creates a negative state and unresourceful physiology. Unconscious confusion tends to happen far less frequently than most coaches suspect.

Conscious confusion, on the other hand, is incredibly useful. In these instances, the conscious mind is striving to make sense of the situation or what is being asked of it while the unconscious mind either already understands or is deeply enjoying the process. You'll know your client is in conscious confusion because he will say he is confused, yet, at the same time, his physiology will express something quite different. The client's physiology is congruent, and he is showing the signs of a positive state. In these moments of confusion, the conscious mind is busy trying to make sense of what's happening, and the door is wide open to give direct hypnotic suggestions to the unconscious mind. You can create confusion trances in which it becomes very easy to create amnesia direct suggestion.

Revivification

Just as you help the client bring to life the memory that was reprinted, you can also help her bring back to life instances of naturally occurring amnesia. It could be such experiences as waking up in the morning and at first recalling the dreams from the night before. As the morning goes on and things in the outside world become more interesting and important, the dreams fade from awareness. Another classic version of this is coming home and putting down your keys and then forgetting where you left them. The secret here is to either use experiences that the client has already told you about that are personal to her or to use more universal instances of naturally occurring amnesia. As you revivify the experience, feel free to use embedded suggestions and direct suggestions to amplify the effect.

Fractionation

Fractionation is another great way of inducing amnesia. To utilize this technique, bring the client in and out of deep trance a number of times after he thinks the work is finished. As you do this, give a number of direct and indirect suggestions about forgetting the things that the conscious mind doesn't need to hold while the unconscious mind can integrate all the learnings made.

Nested Loops

Nested loops are a traditional NLP tool for amnesia. This approach typically relies on the telling of multiple stories (loops). You begin one story then, as you get close the climax of the story arch (when there will be maximum curiosity), break from that story and begin the next story. Repeat until all of the loops are open. Once they are, do the reimprinting (or any other change process) in the middle, and then close the most recent story first. Next, close the story that was immediately before the most recent story, and repeat until the first story is closed. The idea here is that the conscious mind is fascinated by the stories and desires completion so much so that the listener forgets about what takes place in the middle. In psychology, this is the Primacy and Recency Effect.

(H)NLP extends this beyond just stories. You can think of a nested loop as being a journey through different states. You can create, for example, a nested loop that contains stories, suggestions, novel experiences, and Markov chains. Just as with traditional nested loops, it's essential to remember to close the loops (unless you are leaving one open for a specific reason). You can think of the whole session as being the span of time during which you present the nested loop with the deepest change work right in the middle.

Suggestion

Throughout the reimprinting and amnesia process, use a tremendous amount of suggestion. These suggestions—sometimes direct and other times indirect—are embedded in the stories being told and the processes in which the client is engaging.

When you use suggestion to induce amnesia, it is often beneficial to take an indirect approach. The direct approach is to instruct the client to forget. This, in my experience, has little success, as it puts too much conscious attention on what is meant to be forgotten. Instead, direct the client's attention to the things that are important to remember.

For example: If you are familiar with stage or street hypnosis, when doing an amnesia routine where the volunteer is supposed to forget a number (for example, 7), the hypnotist counts a number of times from 1 to 10 skipping over 7. During this time, the hypnotist gives suggestions around how important it is to pay attention to all of the numbers between 1 and 10. Of course, the hypnotist leaves out 7 each time. The suggestion for amnesia is indirectly given through the focusing of attention elsewhere and the emphasis on the importance of remembering 1, 2, 3, 4, 5, 6, 8, 9, and 10.

Technique 2: Reimprinting Implicit Memories through Explicit Memory Creation

The reimprinting of procedural memory is far broader than reimprinting of episodic memory. Almost any technique aimed at changing unconscious behavior could be considered a procedural memory reimprinting.

For example: A six-step reframe, which looks for the underlying positive intention behind the behavior and then uses the intention to generate new, more resourceful behaviors, is a standard go-to for unconscious behaviors, such as nail biting, compulsive snacking, and smoking. If we take a wider view of reimprinting as the reconsolidation process of memories regardless of technique, then any NLP pattern that fits in this category will apply.

The process presented here does not look like a typical reimprinting because it uses memory in an unusual way and relies on conscious repetition. This strategy, when implemented in the case of OCD, has been documented scientifically to have the same positive long-term effect on the brain as pharmacological therapy does.

Case Study: Obsessive Compulsive Disorder

A common example of the need to reimprint implicit memory is the client who comes to coaching for OCD. While the exact mechanism for this disorder is not known, a number of hypothesis are available. Two come from the work of two leading neuroscientists, Bon-Mi Gu and Keshav Kukreja (*Frontiers in Integrative Neuroscience*, 2011; 5:38). Gu and Kukreja explored the interactions between explicit and implicit memory in OCD patients compared to a healthy control sample over a number of previously published experiments. While it is known that OCD patients have deficits in implicit memory encoding, the relationship between implicit memory encoding and OCD were not clear.

Gu and Kukreja suggested that the phenomenon of *memory mixing* is at the heart of the issue. Memory mixing is the process through which a person relies on previously encoded automatic behaviors so that less energy is required for the encoding of the current event.

For example: A musician who plays the piano and begins learning drums will perform better than a novice because of his implicit memories around rhythm, tempo, and performance of music. The precision of performance will be high while accuracy will be low since the musician must still learn how to play the new instrument. The acquisition of the new musical skill is the result of memory mixing. Implicit memory aids in the encoding of explicit memory.

In the case of OCD clients, the researchers' hypothesis was that it is connected to either a deficiency in memory mixing or overactive mixing. They suggested that clients can compensate for this through hippocampal-dependent explicit knowledge, in other words, episodic and semantic memory formation to aid the implicit learning and help overcome the implicit deficits around handling uncertainty.

The primary example of implicit memory reimprinting via episodic memory can be found in the work of psychiatrist Dr. Jeffery Schwartz. I present a form of reimprinting here built on Schwartz's structure. Although this technique was primarily developed for use with OCD patients, it can be used in any situation where implicit memory is at the root of the problematic state and behavior.

Step 1: Relabel

The first step of the process is to acknowledge thoughts, feelings, and behaviors for what they are. When a client is in a negative state, that state colors her actions, thoughts, beliefs, and values in that moment. When the client is caught up in this, it's very difficult for her to think about the situation logically. She acts primarily from emotional responses generated in the limbic system. The limbic system contains a number of brain areas, including the amygdala, the flight-or-flight response, and the hippocampus. When the client is in the negative states, the hippocampus is busy creating new memory engrams, which makes this a perfect time to create new useful memories. In these moments, the client does not have access to objective thinking or other resourceful thought processes.

If, however, the client is given a new strategy for when she is in the unresourceful state, the opportunity opens itself for change.

The first step of this is to help the client recognize the emotions and behaviors for what they are. In the original Schwartz protocol, he taught OCD patients to relabel their states and behaviors as obsessions and compulsions. The statement might be as follows, "I don't think or feel X… . I'm having an obsession that X… ." In the statement, Schwartz is helping the patient to create a little bit of breathing room with the first half of the statement and then label the states and behaviors as what they are.

When we work with clients with issues other than OCD, we can run the same steps by teaching clients the 60-second rule. Emotions last in the body for only about 60 seconds. If they last longer, it is because the client is doing something in his mind to keep them going. So the relabeling statement here might be something like, "I am having a physical sensation in my body that I call an emotion, and it lasts for only 60 seconds."

A statement like that reminds the client first to get in touch with the physical experience in the present moment and then reminds him that, as long as he stays in the moment, the emotion will subside quickly.

Step 2: Reattribute

This step is focused on reframing the problematic state and behavior. In Schwartz's work with OCD patients, he talked about this step helping to rewire the striatum, the part of the brain responsible for smooth transitions between behaviors. For coaches, this step is very interesting on the level of identity. This step is designed to separate the identity of the person from her thoughts, feelings, and behaviors.

One of the common problems that clients see us for is a confusion of logical levels (**Korzybski**). *For example*: A client could mistake feelings and behaviors for identity. Even if this isn't the cornerstone of a problem, oftentimes clients create meta-problems around the connection between how they are thinking and feeling and the vision of who they are.

Reattribution allows us to separate those out creating a level of dissociation between the client and her states and behaviors. In Schwartz's work, he would have patients remember a short statement, such as "It's not me; it's my OCD." This separates who the patient is from the biochemical process happening in the brain.

In coaching, we have more options. We can use a similar statement, such as "It's not me; it's just a wash of biochemicals." This and similar statements help clients to separate identity from the issue, and it indirectly helps them to denominalize the problem. This means the client, for example, can no longer say I am anxious (or any other problem) because now he recognizes that what he, at one time, thought was a static problem is actually a process that has a beginning and a very distinct end.

The traditional Schwartz pattern relies heavily on verbal expression to change states and behaviors. We know, though, that the words are only one part of the experience. Clients also have the ability to create unresourceful and resourceful images. At this step, guide the client to change the submodalities of any negative internal images so it diminishes the emotional charge. Once there is a positive state shift, lead the client to building up a compelling internal image of himself.

When I work with OCD clients, at this stage, I do something because they are not accessing memory in the same way others do. If you pay attention to the eye accessing of someone experiencing the obsession right before the behavior, that person accesses visual construct instead of recall. At this stage, begin by simply directing the eyes into visual recall. Wait until the client accesses the memory of already completing the task that she was about to become compulsive over.

Step 3: Refocus

Step 3 helps the client to step into a more resourceful behavior and state. In Schwartz's original model, this step is similar to the creation of a procedural memory. However, instead of relying on anchoring behavior, the conscious mind helps create an episodic memory by choosing an activity the client enjoys. It doesn't matter what is chosen as long as the client can participate in it long enough for the state and behavior to reset.

At this stage, coaches can leverage the power of gratitude. There is a tremendous amount of research about the power of gratitude to change the brain. The client, at this stage, will have a positive internal image of himself. It doesn't matter what beliefs the client had around that image because gratitude will automatically change how the client relates to that representation. Have the client write down 5 to 10 things about himself that he is grateful for. The key is that he can write it down only when he begins to feel that gratitude. Depending on the client's self-esteem, you may need to take the lead at first. This is a wonderful opportunity to reframe the problematic behaviors and states as well.

Step 4: Revaluing

This final step is the result of the repetition of the previous three steps. The brain will automatically revalue the states and behaviors. In the original model, this meant that the brain would eventually decide that the OCD behavior was no longer worth engaging in. It was an ineffective waste of time and energy.

It is interesting to note that all of these steps in the traditional approach are focused on negation and passively taking away the symptoms. We know, however, that nature abhors a vacuum, and we can be more active in the process. If one thing goes away, it needs to be replaced with something else, and the client can have some choice.

After Step 3, the client will be in a positive state. As she is in this positive state, elicit three or four values. Remember that a value is an Ad->K+ synesthesia—meaning a *word* that makes you *feel* good. Elicit each value one at a time, waiting to see the positive state. As you go through the values, suggest that the client, in whatever way is appropriate, send that value into the old way of being. She may even want to watch a memory of the problem and send the values into it. The key here is that the values must elicit strongly positive states.

The goal with this pattern is iteration. Schwartz's clients took six months of daily practice to achieve their change. Our clients can be quicker as long as the process is repeated enough times that the problem is blown out.

Reimprinting Implicit Memories through Metaphor

On occasion, clients have an implicit memory that is ready for reimprinting, but no explicit memory is attached to the memory. It's almost as if the implicit memory is floating around with no way out.

This final approach comes from John Overdurf's work and is based on two key understandings:

1. All explicit memory can be metaphor (as discussed in chapter 4).
2. The unconscious mind will produce the most appropriate metaphor to create lasting positive change.

Point 1 will be very familiar to you by now. In other forms of reimprinting, we might suspect the metaphor (explicit remembered event) to at least be tangentially related to the problematic state and behavior. In this version of reimprinting, we are not concerned whether there is an overt connection between the remembered event and the state and behavior.

The second point builds on the first. This form of reimprinting is an open invitation for you and your client to trust the wisdom of the unconscious mind to create powerful change.

On a neurological level, whatever explicit memory pops up will be the right one. We not only are trusting the unconscious but also assuming that the memory/metaphor is in some way linked up to a neural network connected with the implicit memory.

This pattern is done when the client either physiologically regresses or has an emotional reaction that is out of proportion and she is unable to access a memory linked to her current state and behavior. In these cases, the actual event may not have been properly encoded, and the only thing remaining is the state and behavior. In these cases, we need a proxy memory that will allow the implicit memory to finally be released.

Step 1: Elicit the Memory

In instances where this type of reimprinting is indicated, the client will already be in the state and exhibiting the associated behaviors. It is important that you, as the hypnotist, are comfortable with being direct at this stage and suggest to the client that these feelings are linked to a memory and in a moment that memory will appear. Take the time to reassure the client that whatever memory comes to the surface is the correct one for the unconscious to make this change.

At this point, your client will need a point of transition so that the unconscious has the space to choose the appropriate memory. A direct and easy way to facilitate this is as follows:

> In a moment, I am going to count from three down to
> one, and when I reach one, you will find yourself in
> that new memory: three ... two ... one.

From here, stabilize the memory in the client's awareness. You can do this with orienting questions, for example:

- Are you inside or outside?
- Are you alone or with others?
- Is it daytime or night?
- What's happening right now?

Step 2: Dissociating

Once you have a memory to work with, and you have layered up suggestions that this memory is the right one to make positive lasting change, dissociate the client from the event. This is done through the same process as is detailed in previous chapters.

Step 3 and Step 4: Associating into Resources and Gifting

The remaining steps of the pattern are the same as with a standard reimprinting. Guide the client into resourceful states, and the client will then gift those resources to the players in the memory.

Once the reimprinting is finished, test the change. Introduce the anchors for the old state and behavior, and see if the new resourceful states emerge. The key to success with this pattern is in helping the client to trust his unconscious mind and to appreciate the fact that whatever memory comes up is the appropriate one for the change.

Chapter 18
Conclusion

If you were to rewrite your past, what would you write? If you could direct the film of your life, what plot lines would you change so that your future was exactly how you want it to be? These are the types of questions we ask of our clients when they step back through time. It is my hope that the answers to those questions are even bigger than what may have been imagined at the start of this book.

Reimprinting is a powerful and fun modality for transformation. At its heart, it is a technique that allows the client to rewrite her past in a way that forever alters her future. Reimprinting makes it easy and safe for practitioners to help clients through emotional issues that in the past seemed insurmountable. As long as the practitioner fully understands all memory is a metaphor and reality is construction, it becomes easy for clients to move beyond their old limitations.

Reimprinting can take on many forms—from the most obvious versions to forms that reimprint behaviors or help to generate new learning. Helping a client step back through time not only allows him to break free of old problems but also creates an opportunity to format the unconscious mind in ways that make future learning and success easy, natural, and fun.

As neuroscientists learn more about how memory works and the interactions between explicit and implicit memory systems in the formation and maintenance of problems, the various reimprinting techniques will evolve. It certainly appears that the more knowledge neuroscience gains, the more open the discussion becomes between hypnotists and scientists. Ultimately, it is our clients who benefit.

Other Books In This Series

The Swish
By Shawn Carson and Jess Marion

The Visual Squash
By Jess Marion and Shawn Carson

The Meta Pattern
By Shawn and Sarah Carson

The BEAT Pattern
By Shawn and Sarah Carson

The CIA Pattern
By Sarah Carson and Shawn Carson

Other Books By This Publisher

Deep Trance Identification: Unconscious Modeling and Mastery for Hypnosis Practitioners, Coaches, and Everyday People
By Shawn Carson and Jess Marion with John Overdurf

Deep Trance Identification Companion
By Shawn Carson and Jess Marion with John Overdurf

Quit: The Hypnotist's Handbook to Running Effective Stop Smoking Sessions
By Jess Marion, Sarah Carson, and Shawn Carson

Keeping the Brain in Mind: Practical Neuroscience for Coaches, Therapists, and Hypnosis Practitioners
By Shawn Carson and Melissa Tiers

Tree of Life Coaching: Practical Secrets of the Kabbalah for Hypnosis and NLP Practitioners and Coaches
By Shawn Carson

I Quit: Stop Smoking Easily Through the Power of Hypnosis
By Jess Marion, Sarah Carson, and Shawn Carson

From Call to Client
By Jess Marion, Sarah Carson, and Shawn Carson

HypnoGames for HypnoJunkies
By Sarah Carson, Shawn Carson, and Jess Marion

Small Thoughts for Big Change: 21 Beliefs to Create Magic in Your Life
By Sarah Carson, Shawn Carson, and Jess Marion

The Reality Distortion Field: Change the World by Convincing Others to Share Your Dreams
By Shawn Carson

Have Mercy: 21 Tales to Trance-Form Your Life
By Mercedes Herman